Praise for *Missi*

"The stories [Wills] uncovers are remarkable: touching, tragic, terribly human . . . Her book, written with care, wit and vulnerability, shows that ordinary tragedies deserve our anger and attention too."   —Laura Hackett, *The Times* (London)

"Not just a vivid, compelling account of Clair's family and ancestry, but an intriguing snapshot of Ireland's social history . . . Rigorously researched . . . Empathetic."
                    —Tanya Sweeney, *Irish Independent*

"[Wills] performs a kind of delicate archaeology on the very concepts of familial and historical knowledge . . . Frank, self-aware, and deeply moving, *Missing Persons* draws attention to what (and who) gets forgotten and left out of history."
                    —Jenny Hamilton, *Booklist*

"Fascinatingly, viscerally haunting."
                    —*Kirkus Reviews* (starred review)

"A devastating reckoning with cruelty and conformity."
                    —*Publishers Weekly*

"A stunningly eloquent exploration of how truth-telling, secret-keeping, and outright lies are part of all family stories—indeed, the stories that unite all communities—and how truths, secrets and lies can both protect and destroy us."
                    —Jeannette Walls, author of
                    The Glass Castle and *Hang the Moon*

"Clair Wills retrieves from time's abyss a speculative history of universal import. This is a penetrating and affecting study, essential reading for anyone who seeks to understand the profound contradictions, the secrets and lies, that define post-famine Ireland."   —Paul Lynch, author of *Prophet Song*

"This extraordinary, utterly gripping book reads like a thriller and offers the satisfactions of a mutigenerational novel. Memoir, social history, detective story, ghost story: the singular weave of *Missing Persons* is brilliantly animated throughout by Wills's distinctive ethos, a kind of impassioned, rigorous, open-hearted attentiveness. [She] refuses the 'enormous condescension of posterity' (as E.P. Thompson put it) and turns the white heat of her moral intelligence toward this rich and vexed inheritance."
—Maureen N. McLane, author of *What You Want*

"This is a history shaken by intimacy—a brave and rigorously humane book."   —Seán Hewitt, author of *Rapture's Road*

"Written with elegance and erudition, *Missing Persons* is an extraordinary, moving achievement."
—Doireann Ní Ghríofa, author of *To Star the Dark*

James Stittle

CLAIR WILLS

Missing Persons

Clair Wills is the King Edward VII Professor of English Literature at the University of Cambridge. Her books include *Lovers and Strangers: An Immigrant History of Post-War Britain*, named the Irish Times International Nonfiction Book of the Year, and *That Neutral Island: A Cultural History of Ireland During the Second World War*, winner of the PEN Hessell-Tiltman Prize, among other works. She is a frequent contributor to the *London Review of Books*, *The New York Review of Books*, and other publications. She lives in London.

Missing Persons

MISSING PERSONS

or, My Grandmother's Secrets

CLAIR WILLS

PICADOR

FARRAR, STRAUS AND GIROUX • NEW YORK

Picador
120 Broadway, New York 10271

Lines from *All That Fall* and *Eh Joe* by Samuel Beckett are reproduced by
permission of Faber and Faber Ltd

Illustration credits can be found on page 185.

The Library of Congress has cataloged the Farrar, Straus and Giroux
hardcover edition as follows:
Names: Wills, Clair, author.
Title: Missing persons : or, my grandmother's secrets / Clair Wills.
Other titles: My grandmother's secrets
Description: First American edition. | New York : Farrar, Straus
   and Giroux, 2024. | "Originally published in 2024 by Allen Lane,
   Great Britain."
Identifiers: LCCN 2023041345 | ISBN 9780374611866 (hardcover)
Subjects: LCSH: Wills, Clair—Family. | Ireland—Biography. | Women—
   Ireland—Biography. | Unmarried mothers—Ireland—Biography. |
   Unplanned pregnancy—Ireland—History—20th century. | Maternity
   homes—Ireland—History—20th century. | Irish—England—Biography.
Classification: LCC DA965.A1 .W55 2024 | DDC 929.209415—dc23/eng/20231117
LC record available at https://lccn.loc.gov/2023041345

Paperback ISBN: 978-1-250-37192-8

1 3 5 7 9 10 8 6 4 2

For Caroline

A friend has sent me a photograph, taken more than twenty years ago, of her baby asleep on her lap. It's an outdoor scene – a shaft of light, a slab of granite, the varied greens of moss and grass, picnic paraphernalia. Her rumpled shirt suggests that her baby has fallen asleep after a feed. He lies back, abandoned to satisfaction, as she gazes into his face. It is a Madonna and Sleeping Child. But look, she says, he's a little bit dead. And I can't deny that the slumped head and outflung arm say 'lifeless' as much as they say sleeping. Life, death – what's the difference? say the faces of the Madonnas. Their look speaks of their helplessness as much as of their love. They have given birth to loss, and they cannot now undo that fact.

Did you ever wish to kill a child? (*Pause.*) Nip some young doom in the bud . . .

Samuel Beckett, *All That Fall* (1957)

What haunts are not the dead, but the gaps left within us by the secrets of others.

Nicolas Abraham and Maria Torok,
The Shell and the Kernel (1987)

Cast of Characters

The Victorians

My grandmother Molly, born in 1891 in Cooranuller, near Skibbereen, County Cork, Ireland. Died in 1980 a few miles from where she was born.

Molly's brothers and sisters, Thomas, John, Ellen, Margaret, Jeremiah and Timothy, born between 1871 and 1882 in Cooranuller. All except Thomas and John emigrated to the United States in the 1880s and 1890s. My great-uncles and aunts.

My grandfather Thomas – Tom – born in 1877 in Ballybane West, near Ballydehob, County Cork. Died in 1946 a few miles away in Aughadown.

Thomas's brothers and sisters, James, Jack, Stephen, Sarah, Robert and Mary Jane, born between 1862 and 1880 in various townlands near Skibbereen and Ballydehob, including Ballybane West. All except Stephen emigrated to the United States. More great-uncles and aunts.

The post-revolutionary generation

My uncle Jackie, first child of Molly and Thomas, born in Lissaclarig, near Skibbereen, in 1920. Died in Bury St Edmunds, England, 1972.

Cast of Characters

My mother Philly (Philomena), Jackie's younger sister, born in Hollyhill, near Skibbereen, in 1930. She joined her older sister Mary doing mental health nursing training in England in the late 1940s. She met my English father, Bernard, at Netherne Mental Hospital, Coulsdon, south of London. They married in 1955 and she settled in England.

Jackie and Philly's brothers and sisters, Mary 1 (died 1924), Mary 2, Stephen, Thomas, Jimmy, Peggy and Robert (died 1938), born between 1922 and 1936, in Hollyhill and Aughadown. Mary, Thomas and Jimmy all went to England.

Lily, born in 1936 near Aughadown. Died in 2018 in Staten Island, New York.

The post-war generation

Mary, daughter of Jackie and Lily, born 1955.

My sisters Siobhan, Bridget and Oona, and me, born between 1957 and 1965, in Coulsdon.

My eight cousins, children of my uncle Jimmy and Dot, and my aunt Peggy and Charles. Born between 1960 and 1976, in Skibbereen, Ireland, and in Nottingham, England.

The next generation

My children Jacob (1989), Luan (1993), Thaddeus (19–20 June 1996) and Philomena (1999). Born in England.

Their many cousins, born in England and Ireland, between the 1980s and the 2000s, to people who were married and people who were not.

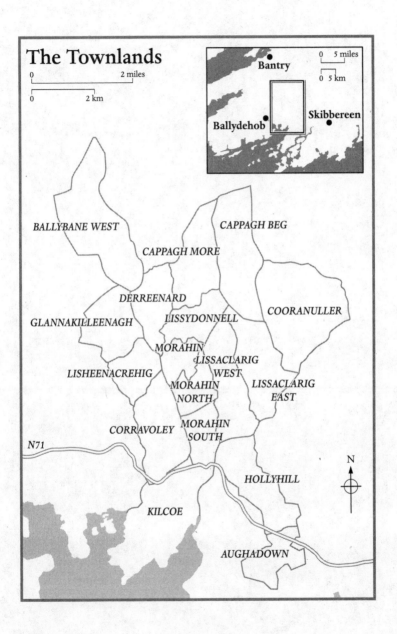

The Townlands

0 —————— 2 miles

0 —————— 2 km

0 — 5 miles

0 — 5 km

Bantry

Ballydehob

Skibbereen

BALLYBANE WEST

CAPPAGH BEG

CAPPAGH MORE

DERREENARD

COORANULLER

GLANNAKILLEENAGH

LISSYDONNELL

MORAHIN

LISSACLARIG WEST

LISHEENACREHIG

MORAHIN NORTH

LISSACLARIG EAST

CORRAVOLEY

MORAHIN SOUTH

N71

HOLLYHILL

N

KILCOE

AUGHADOWN

Contents

Inheritances

I.

I think of history as a long line of bodies, stretching back through time, a bit like those evolutionary diagrams of apes standing straighter and growing taller as they evolve into humans. I know evolution is actually a series of branches, rather than a straight line, but the straight line is, well, so nicely straight. *Homo erectus*, *Homo neanderthalensis*, *Homo sapiens*, all descended from little Lucy. But my figures are all women, heavy with child.

There's my mother on a South London street, in a collarless green tweed coat she made herself, cut in an A-line from the shoulder. It hides her bump nicely but better still it will keep her warm through the fiercely cold early months of 1963 as she takes me to the baby clinic to be weighed, and to collect the free milk and orange juice for my older sisters. She looks un-believably stylish. Her dark hair is cut short and close to the nape of her neck. She has a stack of paper patterns (McCall's and Butterick and Vogue) from which she conjures the most up-to-the-minute designs: a close-fitting waisted dress with the hemline above the knee, a smock with a rolled collar, a Jackie Kennedy jacket, a Jean Shrimpton miniskirt. In a few years I will be watching the little shell-shaped bobbin shuttling back and forth in the sewing machine, picking up the thread and fas-tening down the stitches, and she will try to teach me how to thread it. But for now I'm held firm under the coat.

Behind her stands my grandmother, heavy with my mother. It is the spring of 1930 in the West of Ireland and she is putting up with no nonsense. This is her sixth pregnancy in ten years and she has already buried one child. There will be more pregnancies and more burials to come. The small children tumble and fight around her and God knows where the eldest is – he has taken to heading off out to avoid being landed with another task. He's away somewhere experimenting with trapping rabbits, or dangling a worm on a piece of string to see if the fish in the stream will bite. The labourer's cottage is far too small for a family of seven – eight, including my great-grandmother, who is in her eighties and mostly sits propped by the fire, poking the embers and moving the pots around – and there is definitely neither space nor time for a sewing machine. My grandmother mends her old dresses, and darns her elbows, and knows to make things last. Her luxuries are a plug of tobacco, a swig of brandy in a china cup, a fine black hat, and good quality footwear. Every Christmas, after her daughters go away to work in England, she'll get sent a new pair of Morlands ankle-boots – lined with sheepskin and fastened with a zip instead of laces – and she'll wear them summer and winter, till the next year. She doesn't do seasonal dressing. Decades later, in the 1970s, I will share a bedroom with her in the summers and I will watch her dressing in the mornings. Her clothes have hardly changed at all over the years: the suspenders and worsted stockings, the layers of petticoat and woollen skirt, the thick, long-sleeved blouse even in August, the boots. By then she will have inherited her mother's place by the fire. But in this image from 1930 she is pregnant with my mother, and she spends much of her day outside – with the chickens and the sow, the milker and the small patch of potatoes, or endlessly fetching water. Her back is aching. She's definitely tired-looking, carrying that new baby around.

Her own mother is a good deal more indistinct, standing

behind her in my personal lifeline. She's carrying my grand-mother in the early 1890s, her thirteenth pregnancy – plenty of burials. If I look up images of West-of-Ireland women in the 1890s this is what I find: wary-looking figures standing outside whitewashed cottages in full woollen skirts and shawls. Always an apron. The guarded expressions are part of the charm – they wouldn't look half so picturesque if they appraised the man behind the camera. The photographs are black and white so I can't see the carnation-red petticoats apparently beloved in the West. And I'm guessing that my great-grandmother had little time for dyeing hers. I know very little about this woman – I know that this late baby will be her last and that by rights she's already too old to do this again. She was born in the early 1840s, when the population in West Cork (indeed, in all Ireland) was teeming. I know that her first language was Irish, and that she learnt English as a child – though she never learnt to read and write so I don't think that she got her English in school. I know that by her fifth birthday the potato crop had failed for several years in a row. I can be pretty sure that by the time she was ten she had suffered the effects of malnutrition, and had witnessed starvation and the deaths of relatives and neighbours from typhoid, typhus, diarrhoea and a host of other diseases that thrived among people who hadn't enough to eat. She didn't play. Reporters on the famine in West Cork made a point of noting that children no longer played games, and who can wonder?

She'll have seen, even if she couldn't quite understand, the cabins around her emptying of people. They went to the work-house in Skibbereen in their hundreds, and over six months in the winter of 1846–7 more than seven hundred died there, of starvation and disease. Or they went to Cork City, looking for work or charity and a passage to America. The small townland where my mother grew up is an area of about 200 acres. This land supported twelve families in the mid-nineteenth century; they were reduced to five by the end of it. The parish holds the dubious distinction of being the source of a letter, written in January 1847 to the Relief Committee of the Society of Friends, describing the area as 'one mass of famine, disease and death'. The dead were wrapped in calico and taken to the churchyard in a reusable coffin with a trapdoor bottom. Mass graves, unburied bodies dismembered by dogs and rats, the living crawling in the dirt: my great-grandmother will have seen all that. And she'll have seen the desperate measures taken by those determined to survive – of whom she was one. Nearly a quarter of the population of Cork in 1841 were gone ten years later; but she held on. In 1870 she married a small farmer whose father had managed to keep hold of, or get hold of, 10 acres of land. Where there had once been eight or ten families, now there was one.

And further back, to my great-great-grandmother, I can't see – I can only imagine. She must have been born around 1810, give or take a few years. I don't know whether she had other children and whether they survived. I don't know whether she outlasted the Famine, or whether she figures in those statistics of death by starvation and disease. I know that she cared for my great-grandmother sufficiently well for her to grow up and give birth to my grandmother, and so, indirectly, to my mother and to me.

All the shawls and aprons and worsted stockings say 'tradition', but so much of what happened to these women happened because of the ebb and flow of money and markets. Famine, land-hunger, war, emigration – they were all the consequences not of Ireland's distance from industry and commerce, but its proximity. The common task for all these women was to keep life going, through conception, gestation, childbirth, breast-feeding, child-rearing, domestic work, the slow reproduction of everyday life. But even if all those pregnant bodies look like they were doing the same thing, pregnancy and childbirth don't happen outside history either.

We like to think of generations as succeeding one another, in a long and perhaps even orderly line, like the one I've sketched. Sometimes we make the mistake of believing generations improve on one another, as though history were a story of progress, with the old departing, more or less graciously, to make way for the young. But what happens when generation goes wrong? When youth and sex and change are so threatening that they have to be stifled, or nipped in the bud as Samuel Beckett put it in the 1950s.

I keep returning to a story of generation gone wrong in my own family – a mother not married, and a child stifled. This was a crisis that occurred in Ireland in the 1950s, but it was rooted in a history that stretched much further back, and it cast a shadow for many years afterwards. It is an all-too-familiar story of desire, sex, illegitimate birth, institutionalization and emigration. And it happened in part because of the actions of my uncle – who got his lover pregnant and disappeared to England, abandoning her and her child to a mother-and-baby home and an orphanage. And because of my grandmother – who didn't say no.

The story haunts me in part because it seems to come from a different era, Dickensian in its details: abandonment, cruel institutions, itinerancy. But it was still unfolding while I was a child, in the 1960s and 1970s, just as it was unfolding in similar ways and at the same time in hundreds of other families. Not one bit of it turned out well. I would like to go back and ask my grandmother, Was it worth it? Did you regret it? It would be no use, of course. Part of the point of what happened – part of the reason families put up with the institutions, and put up with the loss of their sons and daughters – was not to have to talk about it. And in the end, perhaps, not to have to think about it.

What would my evolutionary line of bodies giving birth to other bodies look like if it included all those who were lost and discarded along the way? What if it included not only the children who weren't considered part of the family because they were born outside marriage, but the men who fathered them and disappeared to England to avoid the consequences? What if it included everybody who was missing? The problem here is not really one of remembering. We are talking about people – uncles, aunts, cousins – whom I wasn't there to meet, or who weren't there to meet me, and therefore I can't remember them. Still, they made their absence felt. I understood very well as a child going 'home' to Ireland in the summers (from our actual home, where we lived the rest of the year and where we went to school, on the outskirts of the London Borough of Croydon) that a lot of the important people weren't present, and weren't talked about, but that didn't make them any less important. Quite the opposite. Perhaps there is something in between remembering and forgetting – something closer to paying attention. Pay attention now. Listen to what I'm telling you. How often were we told that as children? And we did learn to pay attention, to the things not said as well as to the things that were out in the open.

2.

Due to a cascading series of late and last children giving birth to late and last children my family reaches back a remarkably long way in only a few generations. My maternal great-grandfathers were born in the 1830s. Nearly 200 years in a mere four generations. It's a fact that amazes and delights me, although it can only offer the most abstract of links to the past. Not only did I never meet my Irish great-grandfathers, but my grandfather died years before I was born, in 1946, when he was in his early seventies and my mother was fifteen. However, I remember my grandmother well. She lived for thirty-five more years after her husband's death, on the small farm where she had reared her children – and from where she watched them emigrate as her siblings had done a generation before. This time they went to England rather than America: nursing in psychiatric hospitals, labouring on farms, and building the motorways and power stations of England's post-war boom. Through it all she stayed as if rooted to the spot. As a child I thought that that was what it meant to be properly – legitimately – Irish, as opposed to the half-Irish beings we were, growing up in England. You stayed on your farm. I find it hard to picture my grandmother anywhere except in the kitchen, or outside in the yard with the hens, or drinking tea from a clattery cup and saucer in the big brass bed in the room we children shared with her on our summer visits, while my parents slept in the good bedroom. I assume she must sometimes have gone to town, and she certainly went to

Mass. But in my imagination she was attached to the house and garden. They made no sense without her.

The start of the school holidays meant the journey 'home'. A six-hour drive to Swansea and an overnight cabin on the ferry to Cork; a sleepy climb into the car again the following morning for the next leg of the journey, stopping by the side of the road to pee or to let the dog out of the back to run around. As my father turned off the main road up the lane leading to the farm we leant forward in excitement. My stomach leapt and the dog began to bark.

Summer after summer through the 1960s and 1970s this journey was repeated, as my mother took us back to her childhood home. She was cut off from her past in Ireland and part of the point of these holidays was for her to reconnect – a task that became more and more difficult as the years passed. But she also wanted us to get a purchase on her memories, to know her landscape, so that we could reflect her experiences back to her. We knew the walk to the creamery that she took as a child. We knew her neighbours and their children – the children of those who had stayed. We collected a gallon of milk each evening from the farm at the bottom of the hill, suffering agonies of embarrassment faced with the banter of a group of teenage boys and young men – all brothers – in the milking shed; we joined in cutting and collecting the hay (by hand); we made pocket money by walking behind the digging machines and filling sacks with potatoes. Most of all we got to know my grandmother, aunts, uncles and cousins.

If I had had any interest, then, in comparative economics, the lessons of the journey from our house on the Brighton Road in Coulsdon (now demolished in a traffic management scheme) to my grandmother's farm and back again would have seemed simple. England had jobs, which paid wages, and things to spend them on. None of that appeared to be the case in Ireland. There were hens, and therefore eggs. There was a sow, and sometimes piglets. But apart from the piglets the farm didn't appear to produce anything to sell, although there were lots of stories about the things it used to produce. How the wheat from the fields would be taken to the mill and given back as flour; but now there was no wheat and, as far as I could see, no mill. How milk from the cows would be taken in churns on the pony and cart to the creamery each day, and the proceeds used to buy sugar and tea in the creamery shop next door. But now there were no cows to produce the milk, and, after a while, no pony and cart. How my uncle Stephen experimented for some years with growing flax. How they used to fatten turkeys for Christmas. All of it seemed long gone. Stephen still hired himself out for seasonal farming jobs, but increasingly ditch-clearing and land-drainage were tasks taken on by permanent employees of the county council. One of the main sources of income for the farm must have been my grandmother's state pension.

By the early 1970s the small-farm economy had decisively failed, but my grandmother and Stephen had no option but to keep living inside a world that had no future. Their lives outlasted their livelihoods. It was partly because of this that visiting the farm felt so close to enchantment. It could not exist anywhere else, it could not exist for much longer, and somehow, small as we were, we knew that as children.

August was a blaze of red and orange and yellow: banks of crocosmia arching from stone walls covered in piercing green lichens; hedges of fuchsia smothering the brambles; hairy yellow caterpillars and the orange-and-black striped ones that swarmed over the ragwort in the fields. My grandmother, Molly, carefully tended a small bed of flowers dug between the rusty iron gate and the front door that no one ever used (not even the priest or the doctor, by the 1960s). There were blue hydrangeas, and red geraniums with their furry leaves. She had all sorts of cuttings stuck in jars on the windowsill, and was proud of her skill in getting them to take. To me the cultivated flowers looked silly and artificial – which was the point, of course – why try to compete with the brightness of the hedgerows?

She poured tea leaves from the pot onto the flags outside the door (to kill the weeds, she said). But the weeds were getting the upper hand. The fire was lit too seldom in the west room to keep the mould from the walls. Later the damp made the good bedroom uninhabitable too. Our journeys in the 1970s took longer as we towed a slowly swaying caravan behind us all the way from Coulsdon. Its roof curved from front to back, and I thought of it as a snail shell we carried with us, complete with orange nylon curtains. It was parked in the farmyard for the duration of our stay and our parents slept in it.

For the last few years of her life, when my grandmother was very frail, she moved from the farm, which by now was in very poor repair (there was still no boiler in the late 1970s, no bath, and no heating apart from the open fire), to my aunt and uncle's warm and comfortable house a few miles away, where she sat for long hours in an armchair and watched the colour television she encountered there for the first time. She said her prayers during the evening Angelus. She concentrated hard on what appeared to me even then to be gloriously naive advertisements: a still picture of a bag of fertilizer, a new chemical spray for potatoes, or a bottle of red lemonade, with a voice-over urging you to buy. And she was transfixed by the news, which soon came to rival, if not actually displace, her addiction to the local weekly newspaper. She would gasp in distress at every report of death or injury. As a teenager I was confused by her reactions. In those days every road accident in the country was still announced on the national evening news – or so it seemed. It felt a bit shabby not to share in her anguish, pierced as she was by reports of a fatality several hundred miles away in County Louth, but I also wondered: Doesn't she know these things happen? Isn't there a difference between a tragic accident and deliberate violence? I was operating on a rudimentary scale in which big tragedies, like the Cambodian genocide, or violent death in Northern Ireland, trumped small ones, and I assumed that although my calibrations might be imperfect, they were natural and self-evident. But not to her, for whom scale and distance were measured very differently.

Anyone watching her in her late eighties, trying to bridge the gap between a set of experiences and a worldview that had largely been laid down before the First World War, and the newly moneyed entrepreneurial world of Fianna Fáil Ireland in the 1970s, would have felt a tug of compassion. Free trade, foreign direct investment, industrial development, membership of the European Economic Community, even people taking holidays abroad. How could she make sense of it all? I used to wish she could end her days sitting by the fire in her own house, poking the embers and reading the *Southern Star* by laying it on the floor beside her, since she refused to wear glasses to correct her long sight. I didn't know then that the crumbling house was my grandmother's punishment. I didn't know then about the ruinous error she had made twenty years earlier, which had blighted her life and the lives of those around her. I didn't know about the harm she had caused.

There are stories that get passed on and stories that don't. The story of how her eldest son – my uncle Jackie – had got his lover pregnant in the 1950s was not spoken of to anyone in my generation. Sacrifices rarely take place out in the open, and what happened amounted to the authorized sacrifice of some individuals for the sake of others; for the sake of rigid adherence to the 'values' of family, respectability and legitimate inheritance. Such violence had to be hidden. It was not spoken of across the generations, and perhaps it was not spoken of by my mother and uncles and aunts when they were by themselves. But we were all living in the aftermath of a series of catastrophic decisions, whether we knew it or not. And the farmhouse that seemed to me to be the centre of a world was, in fact, a ghostly void. It was where things didn't happen and couldn't happen; a stage-set for a group of missing persons.

Our summers were all about being, and performing, family. However half-Irish I may have felt at the time, my sisters and I were legitimate, literally, and so we were, as the Irish Tourist

Board brochures put it, 'Welcome Home'. In a picture taken in what must have been 1966 there we all are, standing around in front of the porch, my mother, my grandmother, my uncle Stephen and the four of us girls, staging ourselves for my father's camera. We look like an advertisement for an Irish emigrant holiday. My older sisters are both decked out in matching Aran jumpers and hats, one red, one orange. We are dressed up for an idea of a trip to Ireland in the 1960s, yet we are also the reality.

There were other cousins who were not welcome, not recognized, not there. There were other uncles, whom we sometimes heard about in relation to the long-gone world of the pony and trap, the turkeys and the wheat. We never saw them. Who was missing? Why were they missing? Why was their absence condoned? All that I and my sisters and cousins have left to us now to try to piece it all together is a series of belated disclosures, a meagre set of documentary records, and our memories of the stories we were told. The stories – little incidents that have morphed over time into anecdotes, household sayings and family folklore – are our principal inheritance, and they are full of interruptions, encrypted puzzles and loose ends. But the enigmas and the gaps are what we need to learn to read if we are ever to get out from under this history. I'm tempted to say that history has been pressing down on us for far too long. But it's worse than that. It's been expressing itself through us. Reproducing itself, all this time.

3.

The farmhouse and the small fields in which I and my sisters and cousins played, and frequently argued and made up, form the scenic backdrop to this family story, but they are only part of it – only the part we could see. The rest was kept hidden from us. It was taking place elsewhere: in England, and America, and inside Irish institutions, especially a mother-and-baby home and an orphanage, or what was still known then as an 'industrial school'. These institutions were invisible as far as life on the family farm went – in fact that was the point of them, to render illegitimacy invisible. The mother-and-baby homes were religious-run, state-funded institutions where unmarried pregnant women and girls went to have their babies in secret, and from where many of the babies were adopted – often under extreme pressure, and increasingly, in the 1950s and 1960s, to the United States. But the two kinds of home were two halves of one story, and if I am to understand what happened, and how it happened, I need to fit them together again.

The network of institutions for poor and unmarried mothers and their children was not in itself secret, of course. These were usually large establishments, accommodated in former workhouses or repurposed private mansions on the edges of towns. They were funded by local taxes, staffed by religious orders, serviced and provisioned by employees of the county council and sometimes by private contractors. They weren't so much secret as in the business of secrecy – they were places where families could hope to keep an unplanned pregnancy quiet, and so too the existence of a child; and where the members of the religious orders involved in running the homes all too often saw their role as hiding a girl's shame, and perhaps, too, punishing her for it. Between Irish independence in 1922 and 1998, when the last of these institutions closed, they were home (at the lowest estimate) to 56,000 unmarried mothers, ranging from twelve-year-old girls to women in their forties, and at least 57,000 babies and small children. There were similar institutions in the United States, Britain and many European countries: nowhere else were they still in use as late as the 1990s. The proportion of Irish unmarried mothers who were admitted to mother-and-baby homes or county homes in the twentieth century was probably the highest in the world – but this is not the only Irish anomaly. Irish women also stayed longer in these homes than in their European counterparts, with the longest stays in the 1940s and 1950s, when they averaged more than a year.

In the spring of 2023 the Irish government instigated a redress scheme – the Mother and Baby Institutions Payment Scheme – in response to pressure from former residents of the homes (both mothers and children) and groups campaigning on their behalf, for financial recompense for the suffering they endured inside the institutions, and as a result of coerced and closed adoption. The scheme – which has come in for a great deal of criticism for its attempts to save money by excluding some residents from its remit, in effect setting up a kind of hierarchy of suffering – is just the latest in a series of attempts by the Irish government to manage the public shock and anger that has arisen following revelations concerning social welfare institutions run by the Catholic Church, on behalf of the Irish state. It is nearly fifteen years since the Ryan Commission to Inquire into Child Abuse concluded, in a five-volume report, that orphanages and industrial schools run by the Catholic Church in Ireland were places of fear, neglect and endemic sexual abuse. Just over ten years ago, an official report into the notorious Magdalene Laundries found that between 1922 and 1996 approximately 10,000 women and girls were confined and forced into unpaid work in these institutions, and that many of them – particularly unmarried mothers – were sent there by the state.

Unlike the other scandals of institutional life, the mother-and-baby-home scandal started with a grave. In 2014, following painstaking research by the historian Catherine Corless, the bodies of nearly 800 babies and small children – some may have been as old as four or five when they died – were found to have been deposited, over a number of decades, in a disused septic tank in the grounds of one former mother-and-baby home run by the Bon Secours nuns in Tuam, County Galway, in the West of Ireland.

The septic tank discovery became the subject of a series of international news stories that were impossible for the Irish government to ignore, and in 2015 a commission was set up to inquire into the operation of the homes – the Commission of Investigation into Mother and Baby Homes and Certain Related Matters.

The discovery of the bodies of the infants under the concrete lids of the sewer chambers was a horror almost beyond comprehension. But plenty more evidence of the mistreatment and neglect of illegitimate children has come to light, through the testimony given by former residents, the work of survivors' campaign groups, investigative journalism, and the historical research which formed part of the Commission's inquiry. In one of the largest homes, Bessborough in Cork, where local authorities across the country sent unmarried mothers to give birth until the late 1990s (and which also accepted private, fee-paying mothers), more than 900 children died. Over a twenty-year period between the mid-1930s and the mid-1950s approximately 25 per cent of the babies born in the home died there – five times the infant mortality rate for the state in 1950. According to the home's own records a common cause of death was 'marasmus', or malnutrition. These children were in the care of the state, but they were not cared for, and very few of them appear to have been properly buried (there are burial records for only 64 of the 900 babies). As the report of the Commission of Investigation into the homes puts it, 'in the years before 1960 mother and baby homes did not save the lives of "illegitimate" children; in fact, they appear to have significantly reduced their prospects of survival.'

The Catholic homes were a relatively cheap way for county councils to discharge their duty of care to destitute and troubled families and unmarried mothers – the nuns, who ran many of the homes, didn't get paid, after all. And they also provided a means of tidying away the problem of illegitimacy behind closed doors. But as it turned out, the babies were forgotten about inside as well as outside the walls of the homes. The Commission's verdict on the care of the children was scathing. In the face of mountains of archival evidence of the deaths and improper burial of children in their charge, individuals involved in running the homes simply 'forgot' what had occurred. Missing burial books, whole councils blanking out any detail of where hundreds of children were buried, women who had looked after babies for years unable to recall that any had died. In fact, the past has not been forgotten so much as disremembered, indeed dismembered. There is an active element to the refusal, or inability, to remember or to know.

I suppose it's not hard to see why disremembering might feel more comfortable, or safer, than keeping this history in mind. All those dead babies were missing persons. All those missing persons left gaps, of space and time, that had to be filled somehow. Daughters disappeared into institutions, sons went to England, babies died or were sent to America, and families reshaped themselves around the missing. A whole society learnt not to look, or not to look too closely, and certainly not to ask too many questions. A whole society learnt to avoid the shady outlines of the missing people who had once sat at their tables, or hung about in the school playground, or danced with them on a Saturday evening, or knelt beside them at Mass.

When the final report of the Commission of Investigation into Mother and Baby Homes was published in 2020 it caused an outcry, because of its assessment that those who bore the greatest responsibility for the horror and cruelty experienced by so many women and their children were not officials of the Catholic Church and the state, but the women's families instead. Women who became pregnant outside marriage were not forced into the homes, the commissioners argued. Abandoned by the fathers of their children, and by their parents, they had had nowhere else to go:

> Women who gave birth outside marriage were subject to particularly harsh treatment. Responsibility for that harsh treatment rests mainly with the fathers of their children and their own immediate families. It was supported by, contributed to and condoned by the institutions of the state and the churches. However, it must be acknowledged that the institutions under investigation provided a refuge – a harsh refuge in some cases – when the families provided no refuge at all.

Even if this statement were true (and in several respects I believe it isn't), it gets us nowhere. In thinking about this history, it seems to me supremely unhelpful to try to shift blame for the treatment of unmarried mothers and their children onto either the institutional system or onto families, as though they operated independently of one another. It's a way of side-stepping the very thing that needs to be explained. It tells us nothing about *why* a young woman's father and mother, boyfriend or lover, and perhaps too the young woman herself, her friends and her community, consented to the mother-and-baby homes, the orphanages and the industrial schools as ways to manage illegitimacy. Why did people – why did we – countenance all those missing persons? The question that I would like to have asked my grandmother keeps nagging at me: How could it have been worth it? Another way of putting it is to ask, why did it make sense to her – and thousands of others in her generation – to conform to the punishing morality of the system?

I can turn to historical accounts to learn how the network of institutions developed, what they replaced, how they were run, who used them and why. I can read memoirs, testimonies and oral histories to find out what it felt like to be a victim (and even occasionally a beneficiary) of the system. But I am frustrated by a gap in my own understanding. I find it extremely difficult to grasp why, for so long, ordinary people consented to, and even approved of institutions such as the Magdalene Laundries, the mother-and-baby homes, the county homes and the industrial schools. This is despite the fact that some of the people who consented were my own parents, grandparents, aunts and uncles. Or perhaps it is because of that fact. I'm confronted by a kind of disproportion. The chasm between belief systems seems so huge. Only a few decades ago it apparently made sense – as a parent, or a sibling, or a lover – to allow your daughter, or your sister, or the mother of your child to be effectively incarcerated, their baby forcibly adopted or put in another institution. Or it made sufficient sense to tip the scales against the unhappiness people must have felt about destroying their own families in this way, destroying the people they loved. To us, now, it seems pretty much unthinkable, yet the distance between us and the people who believed in the system (or believed enough) is very small. Sometimes there is no distance at all. Sometimes the person who feels appalled by the cruelties of the system and the person who believed enough is the same person.

No one nowadays tries to claim that what happened was OK, or even not so bad. Popes, bishops, prime ministers and presidents have publicly apologized for their involvement, and confessed to their shame. But what's hard, when thinking about patterns of behaviour that have been overturned, is to try to get back to what it felt like to participate in them, and perhaps too to what it felt like to need to participate.

I can consider relative poverty, life chances, rationalization of the available options (presumably nobody went ahead thinking, 'I am destroying the person I love'), the lack of alternatives, the trust in priestly authority, the problem of deference, the premium on 'respectability', the absence of family planning, the economies of farm life, and the general 'precarity', to use an anachronistic but useful term. But none of the historical explanations gets me much further with the near–far problem – the problem that all of this was accepted so recently, including by people I know.

I've been trained to study documents, and to gather information about the past from written records. For years I've written about Irish history by interpreting what's been left behind on paper and in visual records, such as photographs and pictures in magazines. But official reports and documentary histories aren't going to help me work out why people like my uncle and my grandmother acted as they did, why they made the choices they did, and, indeed, whether they felt that they had choices at all. For that I need to turn to a different set of sources, the ones embedded in my own family. After all, this business of the past is also inside me. I'm one of the records in this story, and so are my mother and my aunt, my sisters and my cousins. If I'm going to tell the story in a way that does justice to this past, I need to find a way to read the traces it has left in me, a child born in South London in the early 1960s to an Irish mum and an English dad. A not-quite-fully-Irish person.

Ideas of 'legitimacy' and 'illegitimacy' had long outlasted their social usefulness in 1950s and 1960s Ireland, yet they still had enormous power to dictate decisions about who counted and who didn't. And they may hold purchase still. It's over thirty years since I first tried to find out more about my family's missing persons. I kept asking questions and requesting records and then, after a while, I kept giving up. It became a cycle, of taking up the story and letting it go again. One of the reasons I kept letting go was because of a feeling of illegitimacy. I persuaded myself it wasn't my story to tell. I never knew the people I was trying to trace. Not only that, but I didn't even live in Ireland, I wasn't 'properly' Irish, and it felt like I was borrowing, or even stealing, to think I might have the right to find out more.

More recently I have come to understand that sense of illegitimacy as key to how I must construct my story if I am to tell it right – including my decision to go ahead and have my own first child 'out of wedlock' at the end of the 1980s. I need to harness that feeling of uncertain belonging because it is one part of my inheritance from my Irish family, and in fact it may be an advantage in helping me to imagine what it might have felt like not to belong at all.

This is not a history of twentieth-century institutions in Britain and Ireland, or of a generation 'lost' to emigration, nor is it exactly a memoir of my family's experience. There is too much I don't know for that. It's an account of the past experience of an older generation as it outlasts itself and lingers in the present. I want to understand how the traces of lives that were effectively stopped – expunged from the family, literally buried, or buried alive in institutions – may be read in the lives of those who were permitted to continue: me, and my sisters and cousins. The landscape of the 1890s, or the 1920s, or the 1950s, or even the 1970s that I can manage to reconstruct is full of blind spots, failures of imagination, and vital missing parts. We all know what it feels like to inherit a story, and a set of beliefs, we only partially understand. But we are our own archives. I am convinced that the manner in which we inherit the past – how we know about it and how we think about it, not simply what we know about it – can tell us things about the past, and about the way we live in the present, that we did not know we knew at all.

Half-Lives

4.

My baby's headstone stands taller than everyone else's. I mean this literally – it is a great, solid slab of Hornton stone that dwarfs the surrounding memorials in the graveyard in an almost embarrassing way, given his tiny dates: 19–20 June 1996. There is a practical reason for this mismatch. When my partner and I bought the plot, in those crazed and painful days that June, we learnt that each eight- by two-and-a-half-foot patch of earth can accommodate two-and-a-half people. Better leave room to write in ourselves, we thought. Why waste the space? And I was rather comforted by the notion that I knew where I was headed in the end. But my partner and I are no longer together, and for a long time when I thought of that headstone I imagined instead my parents' names inscribed below my son's, and their bodies lowered into the little plot alongside his small bones.

The huge stone wasn't all about conserving resources, however. It was also a way of insisting on his little life. He died shortly after he was born in the small hours of the morning, in a hospital in Hackney, after I haemorrhaged during labour. When the hospital chaplain came to see me later, I still had Thaddeus lying next to me in the bed, and I asked him to baptize him. Er, no, he explained, he couldn't do that, because he was already dead. He kept fiddling with the little metal paperclip he had used to attach some records to the inside cover of his black notebook. I was out of it on the morphine I had been given for the emergency Caesarean section, and I remember feeling not merely confused but astonished. He was so lately dead! Barely dead at all! Wasn't he still warm? Couldn't he do it anyway? The paperclip went up and down.

Later, the priest from my parish in Stoke Newington turned up and (or at least this is how I remember it) baptized away without any qualms. Or he blessed him, or something. At any rate he made it OK. It wasn't that I had faith; I needed a ritual. After that I went into ritual overdrive. We drove out to graveyards all over London, looking for a plot. I was so recently stitched that I had trouble getting in and out of the car to survey the desolate burial places under flyovers and within hailing distance of the North Circular Road. And we arranged a big Funeral Mass, with all the works – the coffin on a little stand at the front of the church, cousins over from Ireland, readings, poems, hymns, flowers. All this for a baby who had lived for less than an hour, who was born a little before midnight on 19 June, and died a little after midnight on the 20th. I look back and wonder why someone didn't take me aside, although I would have reacted to them as I reacted to the hospital chaplain, with uncomprehending blindness. The whole thing – the big Mass, the big stone, the big family event – it was madness, but it was also necessary.

I wanted my baby to be less dead, obviously. But given that that wasn't an option I tried to make him more present: more real, but also more equal. He was going to get the same as everyone else – if not more. It was rage against fate, and at the time I found it a whole lot easier to blame fate than the doctors who had failed to save him. If it was the fault of the doctors then things might have gone differently, and that was a thought I simply couldn't bear. I was determined my baby was going to count, whatever his fate, and it seems to me, now, that in the background to my desperation lay all the babies that I obscurely knew hadn't counted, or hadn't counted enough. I didn't want Thaddeus to be one of them.

The revelations over the haphazard burial (would dumping be a more accurate word?) of the bodies of the babies and small children in the grounds of the home in Tuam were shocking for many reasons, but high up among them was that they offered incontrovertible physical evidence that some lives mattered more than others in twentieth-century Ireland. Naturally that is not in itself a surprise, although Irish society is adept at pretending that it managed to escape the class system that apparently uniquely marred British society. Its overlords were mostly foreign and Protestant, and were mostly got rid of; it escaped the Industrial Revolution (as though class only arrived with factories); its cities were small and in them community life was still possible; and anyway, through much of the twentieth century no one (not only the poor) had any money. Weasel terms like 'status' have been used instead of 'class' to describe the rigid stratifications in rural, small-town and urban Ireland. But everybody knows there were the haves and the have-nots. Everyone knows that lots of the have-nots went to England, to become the underclass of the post-war industrial boom, to try to make good, or to have their babies in secret. Government officials acknowledged in the 1940s that without the 'safety valve' of emigration the country might have had a social revolution on its hands. For others there were the industrial schools, the county homes, the asylums, the laundries and the mother-and-baby homes. Nearly everyone over the age of forty knows of someone who was incarcerated in one of these institutions, if only for a time. Online sites, blogs, advice columns and chatrooms reveal thousands of people searching for information about their mothers, sisters and aunts, and, weirdly, even about themselves.

They are investigating their own exclusion from society, their own status as missing persons. These are people who know all too well what it is like to live a kind of half-life, somewhere out of reach, cut off from the communities that went on without them, for six months, or two years, or ten, or twenty, and sometimes for a lifetime.

It's funny about the time-lag. It's as though people who were sacrificed to the institutions have had to wait for other people to stop believing in them before they could properly acknowledge – maybe even to themselves – what they had gone through. It had to appear to be safely in the past before they could say, or sometimes even know, this was what happened. This was how my future was taken away from me.

There is an early painting by Giovanni Bellini that hangs in the Metropolitan Museum in New York. *Madonna Adoring the Sleeping Child* dates from the 1460s, and has been over-enthusiastically cleaned and restored so that there is something disturbing about the baby's china-like flesh, picked out in dark outlines, and something definitely off about his impossibly bent right arm. 'The sleeping child is a reminder of Christ's death and sacrifice,' says the catalogue note, and he certainly looks not too well. And then there is Bellini's *Madonna Enthroned Adoring the Sleeping Child*, in which Jesus' arm dangles in a positively dead-child manner. The dead weight of his arm mirrors almost exactly the dead weight of the crucified Jesus' arm as he sprawls heavily across his mother's lap in Michelangelo's *Pietà* at St Peter's. If he is alive, he is only a little bit alive.

One line on the parallel between the Madonna who breastfeeds her baby and the Madonna who weeps over her dead son is that her tears take the place of her milk, as Jesus' life comes full circle. But by rights she shouldn't be crying. 'Since resurrection lies in the offing,' says Julia Kristeva in an essay on the Madonna, 'and since as the Mother of God she ought to know that it does, nothing justifies Mary's anguish at the foot of the cross unless it is the desire to feel in her own body what it is like for a man to be put to death, a fate spared her by her female role as source of life.' This contradiction – we could just call it a gap in time – is short-circuited by the mother who gives birth to a child who dies. Her body bursts with milk and tears and blood. Her breasts harden with unwanted milk and her eyes seep. She puddles, like a stricken Witch of the West: 'I'm melting.' Hers is a body that cannot deny that the source of life is also the source of death. Baptisms, and even funerals – since funerals presume a life has been lived – are one way of repudiating this unwelcome knowledge.

My attempt to persuade myself, and those around me, that my own baby was barely dead at all extended beyond baptism. I wanted him beside me. I wanted to adore my sleeping child, and in fact if you cradle a small dead body close it does stay warm, or a little bit warm. But that brings its own problems. I kept Thaddeus next to me in the hospital bed until one of the midwives – her name was Helen – suggested she take him away and pop him in the fridge for a while. She didn't say that the medics were worried that his body would begin to break down, but that is what she meant. 'Don't worry, I'll bring him back.' Which she did, and over the next twenty-four hours or so he came and went, in his Moses basket. Once, when she arrived to take him off for his chilling I asked her, what kind of fridge? I was imagining him in one of those crime-drama metal drawers. Um, she said, I think it's a Zanussi. It was one of the few really good laughs I got in those days – seeing him suddenly in with the milk and orange juice.

Later, at the funeral, my sons took over the task of keeping him alive. 'Why is it so big?' asked the three-year-old, as, arms outstretched like a fisherman recalling his catch, he tried to measure the difference in size between the box in front of him and the tiny body he had seen. I must have given an inadequate answer – all I could see was how small the coffin was – because several months later he came to me in some distress to say that he was worried that Thaddeus would be getting too big for his coffin now. His older brother had a similar concern. They had each chosen a treasure to place in the coffin: a cardboard version of *The Very Hungry Caterpillar* (I tried not to think about the wormholes), and a soft toy. Wouldn't he be getting very bored by now, with only those toys to play with?

A child who has never really been born cannot really die. It is immortality of a kind, but not the sort that anyone would really hanker after – in a box, underground, just persisting, like the buried bachelor farmer, Paddy Maguire, in Patrick Kavanagh's poem 'The Great Hunger':

> If he stretches out a hand – a wet clod,
> If he opens his nostrils – a dungy smell.

Irish literature is full of images and stories of the undead and the half-alive, from the ur-text *Dracula* (where the Count survives his trip to London by burying himself at night in a coffin filled with earth from home) to the permeable boundary between the living and 'that region where dwell the vast hosts of the dead' in Joyce's short story 'The Dead', to the entire cast of *Cré na Cille*, Máirtín Ó Cadhain's novel in which the inhabitants of a rural village are all confined to their grave plots, to Beckett's Nagg and Nell, rooted in their dustbins in *Endgame*. In truth, being only half-alive is a condition to which many – most – of Beckett's characters have become accustomed.

'Did you ever wish to kill a child? (*Pause.*) Nip some young doom in the bud,' asks Mr Rooney in Beckett's 1957 play for radio, *All That Fall*. The idea that futurity is equivalent to doom is axiomatic for Mr Rooney, for whom any activity at all is a painful reminder of being. Far better to be buried alive in the office:

> And I fell to thinking of my silent, backstreet, basement office, with its obliterated plate, rest-couch and velvet hangings, and what it means to be buried there alive, if only from ten to five, with convenient to the one hand a bottle of light pale ale and to the other a long ice-cold fillet of hake. Nothing, I said, not even fully certified death, can ever take the place of that.

Mr Rooney's existence has been dulled to the point of extinction by bureaucracy and routine, and Mrs Rooney's by domestic life. 'I am not half alive nor anything approaching it,' she assures Mr Tyler. I don't think all these Irish portraits of people who are only 'half-alive' are a coincidence. Writers in the 1940s and 1950s understood there was something amiss with the very idea of family generations succeeding one another naturally over time. There was something badly wrong with attitudes to childhood.

Beckett's notion that nipping a 'young doom' in the bud might be a kindness recurs in Mrs Rooney's story of a psychiatrist's treatment of a girl who 'had never been really born': 'He could find nothing wrong with her, he said. The only thing wrong with her as far as he could see was that she was dying. And she did in fact die, shortly after he washed his hands of her.' The story was derived from a lecture by Jung which Beckett attended while he was in analysis with Wilfred Bion in London in the 1930s. Like the fictional Mrs Rooney, Beckett appears to have been haunted by this tale of a state of suspension between life and death, of life itself as a purgatorial exile from eternity. Who is to say that the fully certified dead have got the worse deal? Like the Madonna, by rights we shouldn't be crying.

It is a fiction, of course, to think of the dead who never made it fully into life as somehow less dead than the really dead. But it is a comforting fiction. The unconsecrated graveyards that dot the Irish countryside (marked as killeens, from *cillíní*, small burial places, on Ordnance Survey maps) are home to unbaptized babies, but also women who died in childbirth, suicides, executed criminals and the insane. In a secular age the natural burial that was forced on these outsiders brings them strangely closer to us – they fertilize the fields we farm, and lie beneath the earth we tread. They are not set apart. It is, unfortunately, far harder to imagine the same of the babies and small children who died at Tuam – most of them aged between thirty-five weeks gestation and three years old – for whom no official burial records can be found. They lie in unconsecrated ground but they do so because they were the victims of institutional neglect, rather than individual tragedy. Yet how comforting it would be to imagine that since the Church and state institutions did not consider them persons – they were not worthy of proper burial – the rules of life and death do not apply. They did not survive, yet they have not gone away.

5.

It was back in the early 1990s, some time before Thaddeus's birth-and-death, that I visited the Convent of Mercy in Clonakilty to try to find out more about my cousin Mary. I cannot remember exactly when I first heard about the existence of this cousin, whom I never met, and who had died more than ten years before I went searching for information. What I knew, or thought I knew, was that my mother's eldest brother, Jackie, had got a neighbour pregnant in 1954. Jackie was then in his mid-thirties and living at home on the farm with his mother; most of his younger siblings were by this time working in Dublin or in London. My mother (nearly ten years Jackie's junior) was doing her nursing training at Whipps Cross in London, and she had to take several months out to go home and nurse her mother who had reacted to news of the pregnancy with a sort of breakdown that everyone called a stroke.

My mother later told me that during those months at home she talked to both Jackie and his lover, Lily, but they would not marry – and that this was in no small part because Lily was never going to be accepted by my grandmother. Lily was from a smaller, poorer farm but my grandmother might have got over that. What she couldn't get over, apart presumably from the fact that she regarded Lily as sexually wayward, was that she also had 'a withered arm'. In the benighted language of biological inheritance that was still current in Ireland, and particularly in rural communities, she was 'poor stock'; it was Social Darwinism that did for her, and would later do for her baby too, putting her at the bottom of the list for adoption, though there was nothing at all 'wrong' with her.

Recently I discovered that Lily's disability wasn't genetic either. She had been a breech baby and her arm had become dislocated at birth. A bone-setter had come – this was the mid-1930s – and he had made a bad job of it. But none of that mattered to my grandmother. Lily's parents were also having nothing to do with their daughter's child. Lily went in to Bessborough home to have her baby, who was born in January 1955 and baptized Mary. Jackie went to work in England, and he never came home again. The farm he was to inherit was destined instead for the second son, Stephen, who came back from Dublin to take over running it.

I cannot remember exactly when I heard this story, but I believe it was 1989 or 1990; I was in my mid-twenties and a graduate student. Nelson Mandela would soon be released from prison, the Berlin Wall had come down, and I had just given birth to my own first baby. My boyfriend and I had agreed on friendly terms to go our separate ways. I would like to think I would have cared about Lily anyway, but I am sure that my shock had in part to do with the frightening difference in our situations. Although I vaguely understood that having a baby on my own was going to be hard (and it was) I never seriously doubted that I could manage the baby, alongside a future job, even future relationships and possibly even future babies (and I could). I did not doubt that I had a future. I felt outrage over my grandmother's behaviour. To destroy three lives (Lily's, and Mary's, but also Jackie's) for the sake of some false – indeed wicked – ideals of morality, propriety and respectability, some bogus notion of genetic inheritance: I could not accept it. My mother's refusal to express the same sense of outrage baffled and upset me. Certainly she expressed sadness, but beyond that I could not penetrate. To my shame, for a time I let the whole thing go.

And it wasn't as though my grandmother hadn't been punished for her intransigence. She had kept the farm, but at what cost? She lost her eldest son; most of the others (two more brothers, two sisters) also lived in England, and came home rarely. How could the house and land possibly have been worth it?

The 30-acre farm was meant to be the crucible of independent Ireland's rural economy, an area of land supposedly large enough for farmers to be able to make an admittedly frugal, but honest and mostly self-sufficient living. Whether that was ever possible is doubtful. One campaigning priest in the 1940s described the life on offer to both men and women on these small farms as a form of slavery. In the 1940s my mother's brothers hired themselves out to local farmers and the county council to dig ditches, lift potatoes and cut hedges in the summers, to make ends meet. Eventually either financial need or a rigid sexual morality, and probably both, was to send them away.

I remember our summers on the farm as idyllic, but they were so in part because the land was barely worked. It made no economic sense to invest in machinery; a visit to granny's was a visit to the nineteenth century. The fields were full of stones, thistles, dock and wildflowers. They were, of course, beautiful. My uncle Stephen borrowed machinery for larger tasks, but mostly he worked with a spade and a scythe. There was a donkey and cart for shifting stuff. He had no car. My grandmother looked after the sow – she seemed to be always making pigswill in the back kitchen. The hens wandered in and out of one of the barns, with its rotted doors and the broken roofslates opening up jagged shapes of sky. I loved the inside of the house: the fireplace with its hook for the iron bastable, the

settle with the horse-hair stuffing coming out, the dresser and low benches painted that particular shade of brown, the blue-and-white striped ware, the pile of copies of *Ireland's Own* to which I brought my puzzled, South London understanding, the daily baking of brown bread, and sometimes sweet white bread with raisins, the enormous (horse-hair-stuffed) mattresses on which we all (sisters and cousins) slept top-to-toe in rows, the cotton squares of curtains sewn on to plastic-covered wire. But the house was rotting as surely as the barns. You could pass a broom handle through the wooden planks that formed both floor and ceiling. One of the three bedrooms was out of bounds as you might fall through to the back kitchen below. And this beautiful but dying farm was apparently too good for Lily.

My uncle Stephen would sit at the long table and pour the

tea from his cup into the saucer to cool it before drinking. In my memory I am always five or six and sitting on his knee. I had no interest then in where he was when he wasn't in the kitchen, or out in the yard giving me a ride on the donkey. And there is so much about him that I do not know. The things that I do know are not enough. I know that he had rheumatic fever when he was a child – my mother recalls how they all had to tiptoe in whispers round the house for months as any sound or movement gave him pain – and he was never physically strong; I know that he drank, though I don't recall him ever being drunk; I know that he socialized in the pub a few miles from the farm and I presume he used to walk there; I know (bizarrely) that he used to poach salmon by setting off small explosions in the river and waiting for the fish to float to the surface. I know for sure that he died when I was ten, and when he was less than fifty years old. I can remember clearly my father taking the phone call from my mother, who had gone back home when Stephen was hospitalized with pneumonia. It was seven o'clock in the morning and we were supposed to be getting ready for school. The tears ran down my father's face.

All this I had stored up when I decided to find out more about my cousin, Lily's baby. 'I cannot remember when' is becoming a trope, but it is the case – I cannot remember when I learnt that Lily had her baby, Mary, in Bessborough Mother and Baby Home in Cork, and that later, when her daughter was perhaps four years old, they moved together to the network of institutions run by the Sisters of Mercy in Clonakilty (a county home, an orphanage and an industrial school). I know now that four years was a very long time to stay at Bessborough, and that the reason for it was Lily's arm. Mary was not adoption material, and Lily could probably find no employment other than working for the nuns. I cannot remember

when I found out that Mary lived in the orphanage run by the Sisters of Mercy and attended the industrial school (until it closed for lack of numbers in 1965 – she may have moved then to the county home) or that she went to England to train as a nurse, that she became pregnant by an Indian doctor, that she went to India to meet the family and was rejected by them, and that she killed herself in 1980. She is buried back in Ireland. I do remember the confusion and distress of trying to piece things together through conversations with my aunt, my mother and my cousins, the guilt I felt about wanting to know more, the sense of a fog of information half-told and half-understood, the frustration of trying and failing to find her grave, and I remember going to the Convent of Mercy in the early 1990s.

I phoned first and spoke to a nun, explaining who I was and what I was looking for – information about my cousin. When had she entered the institution, how long had she stayed there, and was it possible to speak to anyone who had known her? She said she could show me the record of admittance. The old convent – now abandoned and guarded by weeds and wire fencing – was an imposing three-storey, nineteenth-century pile, built on a hill on grounds set apart from the town. More than thirty windows look down on visitors entering the gates. I was terribly nervous as I drove up to the door. I had been at school in England. I didn't know nuns and convents, except by reputation, and that might have been part of the nervousness. But the larger cloud was that I was overstepping a boundary. I did not feel comfortable telling anyone what I was doing. None of this belonged to me, though I felt it touched me deeply. I was an outsider. I felt – and still feel – simultaneously attached to and ashamed of my desire to know.

The door was opened by a woman in black, who looked to be in her late sixties. She introduced herself to me as Sister Immaculata O'Regan. I began to explain again who I was but she put out a hand to stop me. 'I was at school with your mother,' she said. She saw the wild incomprehension track across my face. But she was indeed from the same townland, was brought up in a house a mile or so from my grandmother's farm and had been a few years ahead of my mother in school. It was perfect proof, if I could have understood it then, of the folly of trying to distinguish too sharply between the Church and the local community when making sense of the incarceration of children and young people in Church-run institutions. When one in ten Irish children (the figure is from the mid-1960s) entered a religious life, either as priests, monks, or nuns, what distinction could there be between the family and the Church? What I grasped at the time was that Sister Immaculata – a clear-eyed woman it was impossible not to warm to – was glad to help, because she understood the sadness of the story, and my need to know. I wonder too now whether she also understood the condition of being an outsider. Like me she was both in on and excluded from the secrets of the family and the locale. As we leant in together over the ledger where she pointed out the entry, we were complicit. I do not think I am making this up.

I don't doubt however that had I made the phone call to the convent a year or two later, after the beginning of the public outcry over the Magdalene Laundries and related institutions, I would have been fobbed off. I would have been told that the records were lost, or that I needed permission from some institutional body or other to consult them. I would have been tied up in red tape, as the religious orders closed their doors to callers and instructed their solicitors. And as it was, I got as much evidence as I could bear of the cruelty and lack of love in the system anyway. Sister Immaculata explained that she had not been 'stationed' in Clonakilty (what is the word for the billeting of nuns?) when my cousin lived there, but there was an elderly retired nun, Sister Ciaran, who had known her and who was willing to talk to me. She gave me her phone number. I knew I could not call from my aunt's house or those of any of my cousins, so I used my rudimentary mobile phone, though reception was terrible. I drove around looking for a signal, parked the car on a quiet street somewhere near Enniskeane, and called. Sister Ciaran was in her eighties, living in a retirement home. I imagined myself talking into a small, carpeted bed-sitting room – armchair, TV in the corner, crucifix on the wall. I began badly. A confused and possibly aggressive-sounding account of my desire to talk to someone who had known my cousin was met with a defensive counterblast. It was as though I had got the demonic Mother Superior, played by Geraldine McEwan in Peter Mullan's *The Magdalene Sisters*, on the phone. 'She was a moody girl, a moody girl,' Sister Ciaran said. In another context I might have been able to interpret 'moody' as 'spirited', and tell myself a story of resistance. But I knew, as Sister Ciaran knew, that she had later killed herself. 'Moody' opened up a world of misery on the part of my cousin, and callous indifference on the part of her 'carers' for which I had not properly prepared myself. An already unsteady house of cards came cascading down. I sat back in the driver's seat of the Austin Metro, amid the muck and detritus of the kids (two of them by this time; different dads) – the discarded straws, empty crisp packets, baby wipes, torn colouring books, mashed wax crayons – and wept.

6.

I should not have been so shocked. At the time I was editing an anthology of Irish women's writing, including contemporary journalism, autobiography and memoir. I was familiar with the campaigning articles from the 1970s and 1980s by writers such as Mary Holland and Nell McCafferty on access to contraception, deserted wives, and the abortion referendum of 1983. I knew the stories of Ann Lovett, the teenager who died along with her baby after giving birth outside, alone, in January 1984; and of Joanne Hayes, who was wrongly accused of the murder of an infant later the same year. Both young women had tried to keep their pregnancies secret. Both were scandals not so much of sex and reproduction, as of the various official bodies (the Church, the school, the police and the judiciary), which let them and their babies down. Although the Ryan Report into sexual and physical abuse in industrial schools and reformatories would not be published until 2002, the silence about this systematic torture was beginning to break. There were stories in the papers and on the radio of the pervasive cruelty – rapes, beatings, broken bones – at industrial schools such as Goldenbridge and Artane, both in Dublin, and Letterfrack in Galway. As far back as 1970 the report of the Kennedy Inquiry into children living in residential homes had begun to uncover institutional cruelty and neglect. Ironically the inquiry was the result of conditions improving for children in residential care. They had begun to attract public attention because from the mid-1960s they were enrolled in public primary schools, rather than being educated inside the institutions. This was stuff I knew about – in fact it was part of my job to know about it. But I hadn't really taken it in, and I think now that I couldn't bear to.

Although I cannot remember exactly when I first heard about my lost cousin, Jackie's baby, I can remember who told me. It was my aunt Peggy, one summer when I was 'home' – that is to say, when I was visiting my aunt and uncle and cousins. She told me about the mother-and-baby home and the industrial school, and about Mary going to work in England. She also said that Mary had died in a car accident. It wasn't until later – maybe a year or two later, after I pressed her again – that she admitted it was suicide. And she showed me a Mass card with a photograph of Mary – a young woman with long dark hair and an oval face who looked very like my eldest sister – and an inscription which read, 'All I ask of you is that you will remember me at Mass and Holy Communion.' Then she put the card away again. She was hiding it, but she was also keeping it safe.

The inscription enraged me. Ask more! I wanted to say. Ask more of us! It seemed punishingly cruel that we should have found out about our banished cousin only when it was too late for her to ask anything of us at all. It felt both vitally important, and also useless, to remember her.

And for a long time that was what I knew. A few conversations with my aunt and my mother and my cousins; later, when I had plucked up sufficient courage, a visit to the Convent of Mercy and the conversations with Sister Immaculata and Sister Ciaran.

It's strange the way shame travels. The mother-and-baby homes were supposed to provide a refuge for unmarried girls and a place to hide the 'shame' of their pregnancy. But shame stuck to everything. The shame of sex and pregnancy, the shame of rejecting a child, the shame of being that child who was rejected, the shame of the misery that leads to suicide. Even talking or asking about what had happened felt somehow shameful, but I find it hard to put my finger on exactly why. It is not as though anyone said to me explicitly, 'Just leave the past alone. Why do you want to drag it all up? What good will it do?' But in the great reluctance of anyone to volunteer information I felt it was implied, and since I had no answer to what good it would do, I kept my inquiries as quiet as possible. And because I wasn't being completely open about my search for my cousin, I created something else to be ashamed of. The very act of keeping something secret engenders shame.

For years I've kept a record of what I'm reading in a notebook – a mostly messy mix of book titles, random thoughts and quotations. It's now grown into a long series of notebooks – the closest thing I have to a diary – stacked in a cupboard at home. I can remember where I copied out the ledger entry that Sister Immaculata and I pored over in the Convent of Mercy (this was the early 1990s, before smartphones with cameras). It was on the last page of the black Moleskine notebook I was using at the time. I chose the last page because it didn't seem right to fit Mary in after an account of whatever I was reading then. The record included her date and place of birth, and the date on which she arrived at the orphanage. And working backwards in the notebook I recorded the things that Sister Ciaran said to me on the phone – that Mary's mother used to send her letters from the United States, and the comment about her being a moody girl.

She may have said other things too, but I can't check because I have lost the notebook, a loss that I find both incredible (embarrassing, and even shameful) and entirely logical. I have spent many hours, checking and rechecking through the stack of volumes. First, I turn to the end of each book (there are more than sixty of them) where I'm sure I can visualize the entry. Then I decide I must have made a mistake about writing at the end of the book and painstakingly scan through every page. Then I put the notebook back on the pile and take another. I don't know where it is, but I know it's somewhere. Every few years I go back and try again. It must be there. How could I have lost the book that contains the only tangible evidence of Mary's life at the industrial school? The nuns have packed away the ledgers and I'm surely never going to get to see them again, let alone talk to Sister Ciaran, who must be long dead. But of course it makes sense. How could I *not* have lost it? For years that notebook burnt a hole on my shelves. I had tried to uncover a family secret, but in the process the secret had become mine.

It would be neater if I could tell the story of finding out about Mary as a kind of natural unfolding – gathering and fitting together small pieces of information until something like a picture of a life emerges. But it didn't happen like that. It was all stops and starts and dead ends and subterfuge. And it was not until the public scandal over, first, the Magdalene Laundries and industrial schools, and then the mother-and-baby homes, that I properly understood that what I was dealing with was not only a family shame but a national shame too.

Here again, shame stuck to everything. The problem was that even assuming records of my cousin's time in the Bessborough home, and later in the Clonakilty county home and industrial school, still existed, I had no right of access to them. I wasn't her mother or her daughter or her sister – I was only tangentially connected to her through my culpable uncle, who himself had had nothing to do with her. And as the stories of what went on in the institutions became a public scandal, and access to official documents became even more difficult, even wanting to look for records felt somehow grubby – as though I were accusing the archivists who held them of being involved in a Church–state conspiracy, holding back information they could share if they wanted to. I corresponded with librarians, and archivists, and journalists, asking if any of them could secretly have a look for information. I tried to ask in a way that I hoped sounded like I wasn't really asking. And some of them did help me – that was how I got hold of Mary's birth record, with the informant given as Sister Pilkington, 'Occupier, Bessboro' Hospital, Bessborough', though technically, as a more distant relation, I shouldn't have been able to see it.

So when, nearly ten years ago, the Irish government established a commission to inquire into the mother-and-baby homes – after the dead babies were discovered at Tuam – I felt a sense of personal relief. Bessborough was one of the institutions the Commissioners were going to investigate. I just needed to wait until the report was published and something would be revealed – some missing part of my cousin's life would be filled in.

I didn't wait patiently. The Commission's report on the homes was initially due in the spring of 2018, but it was delayed several times, and finally published only in October 2020. I spent those two years harassing people by email and sometimes in person, which was ridiculous. The report was hardly going to come any sooner because I wanted to read it. The moment the document was published I downloaded it – nearly 3,000 pages of it – and scoured it for information about Bessborough, for what was going on in the homes in 1954 and 1955, for stories about unmarried mothers in County Cork. I read the report as though it was a document about my family.

This was perverse, certainly, but it wasn't entirely misguided. I did find things out.

I read with intensity the accounts of being driven by a relative or a priest or a social worker to Bessborough, with a small case in the boot of the car; the descriptions of the front-of-house parlour where women and girls would have their first interview with the Sister-in-Charge; the stone corridors and the sweeping wooden staircase that mothers awaiting their confinement were required to scrub and to polish, when they weren't doing other jobs such as helping in the kitchens or the laundry, or cleaning dormitories and toilets, knitting and sewing, or bottle-feeding babies in the nursery ('never our own'). I read about the practice of giving women and girls a 'house name', a pseudonym that was used for the length of their stay, ostensibly to protect their privacy, though many people experienced it as stripping them of their identity. I tried to get a sense of the internal architecture of the place. From the outside the house looks like a grand Georgian double-fronted Big House, a kind of stately home (which is what it was originally) with early-twentieth-century add-ons, including a chapel, dormitories and a maternity ward, which was built in the 1930s (before then women gave birth in the hospital in Cork). In the late 1960s they repurposed rooms as additional dormitories, because the numbers of admissions had risen exponentially – in 1971 more than 300 unmarried mothers gave birth at Bessborough, most of them referred by adoption agencies. I recently heard a harrowing story of an eighteen-year-old working in London, who discovered she was pregnant in 1973 and told the aunt with whom she was staying at the time, intending to keep the baby. She was forcibly brought back to Ireland by plane, in the company of a priest, and taken to Bessborough. Her baby was later adopted without her consent.

But in the early 1950s, when Lily arrived in Bessborough – with her small case in the back of the car, driven by whom? Her father? More likely, I think, the local priest; I doubt her father owned a car – the numbers of women admitted each year ranged between seventy and eighty. Still, the home must have been pretty full, as many of these women stayed for at least a year after the birth of their child, and often far longer – either because they didn't have the £100 required to pay for their children to be fostered out, or because they didn't want to leave their babies. A two-tier system developed, separating the girls who were being paid for by the county councils (and who were expected to work in return for their keep), and the fee-paying residents, who were able to leave the home without their babies, while they awaited adoption:

> So, there were the nice middle-class girls like myself, sitting around doing absolutely nothing, we had no occupations. We knitted. We went out for walks on the grounds and we were bored.
>
> We knew that there were other girls in the kitchens and in the laundries and that there were babies somewhere, but it was all very secretive, and we didn't know, and I suppose the whole culture was that you didn't ask questions. You just got on with it.
>
> We were the privileged few and as soon as our babies were born we left whenever we wanted.

As I read through the report I kept trying out bits of information to see if they told me more about Lily and Mary, or not. There's a powerful vignette told by a woman who was sent into Cork City after the birth of her child:

They would have sent us out to buy an outfit in a shop in Cork . . . So you can imagine going into Cork City, buying a little suit, knowing that the suit that you were buying was what he was actually going to be given away in. The thinking behind it is just horrendous.

I found myself thinking, well, at least Lily didn't have to do that, because she knew Mary wasn't going to be adopted. (I bet the nuns left her in no doubt that her own weak arm had put her daughter at the back of the adoption queue.) But as so many former residents remembered, she probably did get regularly scolded and told she was atoning for her sin of fornication, and she was probably offered no care or advice or support – although she was just nineteen years old – and she was probably refused pain relief in labour. She may have breast-fed her daughter for a short while, and sometimes she may have got to hold her while Mary sucked from a bottle – though that was discouraged as it created a bond that was only going to be broken. She got to watch her playing with other children, getting her first tooth, learning to use a spoon, crawling and learning to walk. Maybe she got to cut a first lock of hair. And Mary too must have got to know who her mother was among the adults around her, the ones who were wearing nuns' habits and the ones who weren't. She'd have looked for her coming into the room, and going out again.

It was hard to trace the shadows of Lily and Mary inside the home at Bessborough – hard to fill in the outline of their lives without a single word from them about how they felt, though I could imagine they felt abandoned and angry. But the report was eloquent on what other people thought. The mother-and-baby homes formed one part of a vast bureaucratic machinery.

It reached far beyond the nuns in the institutions, the priests who sought admission for their parishioners, and the bishops who were keen to keep the homes as far from towns as possible and behind high walls. It implicated the local authority employees who signed entry and exit papers, the builders and county council workmen (including the sewage contractors at Tuam) who were paid for the upkeep of the houses and grounds, the health inspectors, the social workers, the doctors and nurses who saw the mothers and babies in hospital if anything went wrong, the priests and nuns working for the Catholic adoption societies, the Gardaí who returned women who ran away from the homes, the pyramid of officials at the Department of Health, right up to the top of the Irish civil service where decisions were made about how to price the mostly clandestine work that the nuns were doing for society: keeping unmarried mothers and their babies out of sight.

Every year the Sisters of the Sacred Heart of Jesus and Mary who ran the home at Bessborough recouped the funds for Lily's and Mary's keep from the West Cork Board of Public Assistance. In the mid-1950s the going rate for a mother was £2 a week, and a child was costed at £1. Later the Sisters of Mercy who ran the home in Clonakilty must have billed the West Cork board in the same way for Mary's upkeep, her school uniform, her schoolbooks. Although my cousin and her mother don't feature by name in the account books, that is where they made their presence felt. Someone had to pay for them – for the whole rickety system – and they did so reluctantly. There were regular wranglings and a long paper trail over the cost to taxpayers of supporting the women and children, including disputes between local authorities over liability, and arguments that a girl's parents should be made to pay, or the father of her child. That must be one reason why my uncle left for

England – he took no moral responsibility for his child, and he didn't want to take financial responsibility either. No one did.

Families and institutions colluded for decades to keep these children hidden, like Beckett's little girl who 'had never been really born'. Across the country, right up until the 1970s and 1980s children born outside marriage were excluded from everyday society, or included only by virtue of being adopted by married couples. It's true that there was a price to be paid by people like Sister Ciaran – who lost her capacity for kindness and humanity working as a functionary inside the bureaucratic machine of the county home and the industrial school and, indeed, the Order. But it was the families – my own included – that bore most of the cost of this bogus division between the legitimate and the illegitimate, between people who counted and people who didn't, even if they didn't recognize it then.

7.

All the people involved in that mess in 1954 and 1955 were condemned to live half-lives – including my uncles. While Jackie
was exiled to building sites in England, Stephen was buried
alive on the farm. And the half-lives lived by Lily and Mary are
all too plain. Beyond my immediate family, however, this tragedy is interesting not for its particularity but for its typicality.
Dead babies, adopted babies, hidden children: every family has
a similar story, and sometimes they even come with happy end-
ings. Tidying women away in mother-and-baby homes or
sending them to England, keeping children in county homes
and industrial schools was the norm. It wasn't secret, it just
wasn't talked about. It was common from the mid-1960s to the
mid-1990s for commentators to remark on the peculiar docility
of the Irish Catholic character – neither fired up by faith, nor
particularly resistant either. The years when Mary lived at the
Convent of Mercy were years in which religious observance in
Ireland was at an all-time high for both men and women, measured in terms of attendance at Mass and participation in
pilgrimages, devotions and missions. The Church provided far
more than a religious home – it provided a social life and a
community.

And then people began to say, Enough. Although the reasons why people stopped consenting to the system may seem
obvious, I think it is still worth asking the question: Why?

Why did my aunt tell me the secret of Mary's life and death?
Was it because she felt it was safely in the past, and could no

longer harm anyone? Or was it a way of bringing the cycle to an end? I had recently given birth to my own first baby, whom I was bringing up on my own, and this may have been a reason why she told me the story of the mother-and-baby home, and the orphanage, and the terrible breach that had occurred in the family. The difference that thirty years made to the outcome of unmarried motherhood was so stark. By then getting pregnant and keeping the baby was almost a tradition in our family. My eldest sister had done it; so had one of my cousins. In fact, throughout the 1980s, these were the only kind of babies born in our family – 'illegitimate' ones. Nobody had yet found a partner and got married.

In 1980, when I was seventeen, my cousin Caroline came to stay with us in Croydon for six months, while she waited for her baby to be born. My aunt Peggy's daughter, she was sixteen months older than me, and I worshipped her, but I think I must have been a sorely inadequate companion for her in what she was going through. She slept in the spare bed in my bedroom and as we talked night after night and the months unfolded, I watched the arc of her belly rising slowly under the covers.

We watched a lot of films on television that spring and summer, including *Rosemary's Baby*, which was definitely a mistake. We lay about for hours on the lawn, sunbathing. We cooked experimental puddings with semolina and spices, and ate at odd times of the day and night. I accompanied her to some of the hospital appointments. The receptionist called her 'Mrs' but in such a tone that I thought it must be obvious to everyone it wasn't true. I don't remember any talk about whether she would keep the baby, or what her options were – though it must have been discussed. What I remember is waiting. A kind of fatalist, resigned waiting.

A few years ago, I read an autobiographical novel called *Motherhood*, by Sheila Heti, about a woman in her late thirties who is trying to decide whether or not to have a baby. She flips coins to get yes or no answers to her questions; she has her cards read; she asks everyone she meets what they think and she's mostly impatient when they tell her that what they think is that she should go ahead. But she's badly stuck. It's as though, she says, she's walked to the end of something, and there's nowhere further to go. A psychic tells her that the problem isn't inside her. Instead, it's bearing down on her from the past: '. . . it may be that you're porous and the grief isn't yours. Does your mother have a grief? . . . you're walking around with your mother's grief and sorrow, and you don't even know it!'

In truth I found the book a bit annoying. So much weighing-up of the claims of writing and motherhood, freedom and responsibility – as though they were different careers, as though books and children were mutually exclusive. It made me feel defensive, because I had put so very little thought into whether or not to have children. Was I so much less serious? Had I placed too little value on my freedom? Had I used having a baby as an excuse not to think?

I realized I was pregnant in the summer of 1988, when I was twenty-five. I was a graduate student. I didn't have a job and, after the pregnancy became known, I didn't have a boyfriend either. I was living at the time in Southampton. In the super-market bewildered old women counted their change with painful care, and on a noticeboard above their bent heads I saw a typed sign saying, 'Pregnant? Worried?' There was a phone number to call for someone to talk to in confidence.

I climbed the stairs to a small office where a woman, not at all like the psychic in the novel about deciding whether or not to have a baby, asked me a series of questions about my life, to which the answers were practical and pragmatic. I said: I'm on my own; I don't have a job; I'm young – but I really meant: I don't know who I am, I haven't started life yet. She said: You're not that young. You'll get a job. You'll be able to manage. It was only long afterwards I realized that the organization was religious, and the woman's job was to persuade me out of having an abortion.

And anyway, it was what I wanted to hear. I thought no more about what I was going to do. I just waited. And I enjoyed the waiting. I liked being pregnant, the arc of my own belly rising. By this time we were a kind of club, a generation of sisters and cousins having babies outside marriage. Five in all, as though we were replacing the people who were missing. As though our mothers had a grief. We were walking around with our mothers' grief and sorrow, just as they had walked around with their mother's.

Yet if that was so, our mothers' grief and sorrow made them determined not to perpetuate the violence. What neither Caroline nor I knew in the summer of 1980, when we shared a bedroom with her soon-to-be-born son, still just a shape under the covers, was that in January of that year our cousin Mary (a person we didn't even know existed) had killed herself and her unborn baby.

It must have been intolerable for Mary to think of that cycle beginning again. The friendlessness. The loneliness. The thought that another child was going to have to go through what she had gone through. That she was going to have to go through what her mother went through.

It is a strange thought that Caroline may have had our cousin Mary to thank for the fact that she was able to escape Bess-borough, and the forcible adoption of her child. We knew nothing about what had happened to Mary, but our mothers knew, and this must have been one reason why Caroline came to live with us. Neither my mother nor my aunt, both born in the early 1930s, one living and working as a psychiatric nurse in England and one bringing up a family and managing a farm business in Ireland, were going to have any truck with places like Bessborough – which was still accepting expectant mothers in the 1980s, and, indeed, still working with organizations such as the Crusade of Rescue and St Anne's Adoption Society to coerce women and girls back from England in order to have their babies adopted. But my mother and my aunt would have nothing to do with rejecting grandchildren. They welcomed them all. And it was around this time that they slowly began to talk about what had happened in the family when they were in their early twenties and starting out on having families of their own by giving birth to us.

For a long time, I thought that my duty to my cousin and her mother was to uncover their story, to refuse to honour the association, seemingly naturalized in Irish culture, between shame and secrecy. It was in this spirit that I made those mostly ineffectual stabs at getting to see various archives, with the aim of finding out 'what really happened'. My conversations with my mother, my aunt and my cousins, and my awkward visit to the convent in the early 1990s were a kind of detective work. But I'm not sure that I have the right to disturb the remains of Lily and Mary any more. I'm brought up short, first, by a sense of my own presumption. Although I would know more, by excavating dates and institutions, would I really know more *of them*? Lily and Mary belong to each other, and to the people who knew them; but they belong to me, and to my sisters and cousins, only indirectly, as lives lived in the dark.

And even if it were possible – even if I had free access to institutional records and letters and diaries – it would not be enough for me to uncover the experiences of Lily and Mary, as though somewhere in there lies the key to unlock the truth of my family. Their lives in Bessborough and the county home don't explain why families – why my family – colluded with these institutions as a way of covering up sex and childbirth. For this I need to understand where the sense of shame and the need to keep illegitimacy secret came from, the work it did for families, and the sense it made. The fact that my family *functioned* despite, and maybe even because of, its missing persons – the fact that it *made enough sense* – is part of my inheritance, and the inheritance of a great many people of my generation.

There is a different set of questions I should be asking of this history. Not, or not only, what happened to the people who were missing, but what happened to the people who were there? How did my grandmother, my mother and my uncles and aunts live with the knowledge of what they had done, what they had let happen? All through the 1960s and 1970s the grown-ups stayed silent about my cousin Mary, who was living in the orphanage down the road. But they knew. They knew about the violence that was being done for the sake of 'the family', and this knowledge was surely unbearable. It had to be hidden from themselves as well as from the troop of us children – we who were also there, and learning to live with secrets.

It is not only what we know but how we know that matters. Those of us, sisters and cousins, born in the ten years after Lily gave birth in Bessborough Mother and Baby Home came of age as a generation obscurely promised to a history we half knew, and the consequences of that half-knowledge were unpredictable. They include the fact that we have had so many babies 'out of wedlock', and have tenaciously held on to all of them. As Patrick Kavanagh put it, we are all 'first cousins to the ghosts of the townland'.

Stories 1

8.

Once upon a time my grandfather got lost on the bog. He was still a young man, not much more than a boy, and he was out in the Kerry mountains, near Bearna na Gaoithe, says my mother. I don't believe her. That's way too far away. Maybe he was on the slopes of Mount Gabriel, or more likely even closer to home in the hilly land on the way to Bantry. Anyway, he was lost, and as the night grew darker and darker he began to worry, and then to sweat. He didn't know where to put his foot for fear there'd be no ground and the bog opening up beneath him. So, he said to his daughter years later, and she now says to me, 'I turned my coat inside out – twice.' And all of a sudden he knew where he was and was able to find his way down.

Of course it makes sense, she says when she finishes the story. You'd have to concentrate pretty hard, turning the thick tweed, the pockets, the collar, pulling the arms through. That's why you have to do it twice. It would calm you down, all that concentrating, so you'd be able to think.

My mother's stories are always like this. You think you are being led into a fairy tale – you meet old men dispensing wisdom, weird sisters, travelling people with rhymes and extraordinary skills with a needle. There are fireside revelations, strange noises, long journeys and death by water. And then she turns a little matter-of-fact pirouette at the end and offers a perfectly rational gloss on her own tale. An air of otherworldly mystery – you expect the fairies to come out from their earthen mound under the hill – hitched to a thoroughly this-worldly account of her parents, brothers, sisters, neighbours, friends: she likes to have it both ways.

I could describe her as a mixture of inheritances, like a character out of a nineteenth-century novel: the folk beliefs and traditions of her rural ancestors, and the years of training in psychological reason, logic and psychiatry. But I'm much more interested in why she tells stories like this. She has turned her past into a fairy tale, an experience pushed so far back in time, and space, that it seems to have happened in another world. It's a way of making it safe. She wants to protect the past from the prying eyes of the present, and the future. And she wants to neutralize its violence. She is frightened that cruelties enacted long ago still have the power to hurt, and keeping silent about her family history, minimizing the violence, or transforming it into a fable, is the only way she knows to keep the future safe from harm. I understand the impulse, but I think it's the wrong way.

'They were Victorians,' my mother once said of her parents. It wasn't so much an accusation as a defence, an argument that they should not be judged by the standards of the present, or even of the twentieth century. She was technically right, of course. They were born on either side of the 1880s, when Ireland was under the Union with Britain: Gladstone, Disraeli, Isambard Kingdom Brunel, bustles, Sherlock Holmes, the Factory Acts, top hats, Parnell, the Phoenix Park murders, the backwash of the Famine – history lessons and clichés crowd in, but the adjective Victorian feels out of place when talking of rural Ireland, even when 'famine' is part of the story.

What she was aiming for was not a chronological truth in any case, but an emotional one. What she meant was that they were Victorians in the 1930s and 1940s, when she was growing up. It wasn't only a comment about Puritan sexual morality – though that was part of it – but about a worldview based on ideas of natural order, duty and deference to authority. Self-fulfilment and even 'individual identity' didn't come into it. Religious belief was part of this worldview, certainly, but given that her father had been brought up in the Protestant Church and her mother was a Catholic, it was not a matter of denomination. 'Victorian' was shorthand for a kind of buttoned-up emotional life and an unquestioned authoritarianism that involved physical punishment of the young, and saw little wrong with excluding those who had 'fallen', sexually, out of society.

Still, it was an odd term to choose, because my grandparents might more properly be thought of as Edwardians, if you are thinking in terms of British history, or part of the revolutionary generation, if thinking in terms of Ireland. One of my grandmother's brothers was killed on the Western Front; one of her distant cousins was the IRA leader Michael Collins, who was just a year older than her. Yet to my mother it appeared that her parents belonged not to the previous generation, but to the one before that. 'Victorian' says, not like us. It is a way of marking distance. But it is perhaps also a way of saying: they were on the way out; theirs was a dying culture. My grandparents and their generation were, whether they wanted to acknowledge it or not, a generation losing out to the energy, opportunities and changing outlook of the young. To my mother it seemed self-evident. Her parents belonged to the nineteenth century and she belonged to the future.

And by the time she was talking to me about her parents their lives really were in the past – the more so because she had left them at home, in another country. The future lay across the Irish Sea. History became geography, as her move to Britain enforced a more complete break with the past. In effect it

pushed the past further back, and it even did something strange to the present. When my mother talked to me, a child of ten or eleven, about her brothers who were working as labourers not far from where we lived on the outskirts of London, I do not think the stories seemed straightforwardly to be about their lives in the present. It felt as though they were happening a generation further back, and very far away, in a world in which eldest sons and youngest brothers were required to undertake long journeys, have truck with strangers, and prove their worth by tremendous feats of strength and skill. All of which was true of course, but their lives weren't really a fairy tale.

I like my mother's stories. She weaves a childhood spell out of loss and nostalgia and the clarity of old-age remembering, and then she administers the grown-up psychologizing antidote.

The family stories are all sewn up, with no space for me, no space for questions. She has built her sense of herself through these stories and at this stage – she's over ninety, and she's definitely packing up her things and preparing to leave – questions aren't helpful. I ask them anyway, my sceptical, disenchanting questions. I go further and I actually check facts, looking up people in the General Register's Office and decennial census, the state's great social-bookkeeping endeavours, one documenting births, marriages and deaths and the other providing snapshots of households in time. Sometimes I come back to her with evidence that proves that what she remembers or what she heard can't have happened that way. She is never pleased about this. Yet she keeps feeding me stories.

Lately, she's taken to telling me a tale about another lost child: a baby born to her mother before she married in 1920. A baby that was given up, or given away, around the time of the First World War. There's definitely something not quite right about this story. It has all the trappings of a fable, but one in which my real-life mother has a walk-on part. The way she tells it, it is mostly set in the early 1940s, and involves a pair of strange sisters who live in a shed, or a shop, miles from the main road, and who impart a secret to my thirteen-year-old mother about a long-lost sibling born thirty years earlier, a secret which my mother never speaks of. Until now – nearly eighty years on.

The story goes like this: during the Second World War, in 1942 or 1943, when she was twelve or thirteen years old, my mother would walk after school up into the hills to a shop that was run by two middle-aged sisters, Maggie and Hannah, who were friends with her mother from way back, from 1910, or 1911. She took with her a pound of home-made butter, which she had stashed in the cool of the church confessional while she set about her lessons in school. The shop was a sort of corrugated-iron shed, and it served the people of a number of townlands living miles from the main road. The moment my mother walked in Hannah would reach for a packet of tea and slip it across to her. The butter was handed over in return. With nine at home, plus a steady stream of itinerant labourers and acquaintances who would sleep on the settle, my mother's family were always running out of coupons, but here they could buy, or barter, off the ration.

My mother's account is full of little details. Once a week, or a fortnight, she would go – the walk took about an hour, and sometimes a boy would pass on his bike and she'd get a lift on the crossbar. Hannah, who had been deaf from birth and made 'strange noises', ran the shop. Maggie was a termagant; no one would cross her. The sisters gave her slices of warm bread and butter. They liked to talk. 'They used to say, Your mother was a lovely woman.' And so the story stutters on, and on, while what initially seemed to be the point – the disclosure of a secret about a baby – recedes further and further from view. It's a story with a hole in it.

Perhaps there was something more specific, which my mother cannot now remember. Perhaps there was a series of clues that she put together with bits of knowledge from elsewhere, sentences she overheard, conversations with others. But all she can now offer as evidence of her belief that her mother had given birth and suffered the loss of a child in her teens, or her twenties, is the recollection of her mother's old friends defending her against imagined slights, and assuring her daughter, 'Your mother was a lovely woman.'

Perhaps this is all she can allow herself to remember, even now. Something was understood in those visits, something unfolded over the year or two that my mother went for the tea and the sugar. And then she forgot it. Or she buried it. And now when it comes to disinterring it, she finds that it's too well hidden. She can't get back to it. It's as though the story's punch-line is missing or can't be said. But even though she has so little to back it up, my mother is holding fast. She is convinced there was another baby.

For the record, I don't believe her. I don't think she's lying but she's not telling the truth either. The truth has got lost, like the baby, inside the story which seems to be a mash-up of con-versations remembered, overheard and misunderstood. I will return to this story later, with what evidence I can muster, but I'm not really interested in whether it's fact or fiction. Instead I wonder why she's so attached to a story about a child dis-covering the sexuality of grown-ups, about a missing person, about a mother's loss, and about a child living somewhere just out of reach – like that old Irish legend she used to tell us when we were small, about the Children of Lir who were turned into swans by their jealous stepmother, and who sang above the lake in human voices for 900 years. Who were gone but still there, if only you knew how to listen.

There's an element of defiance in my mother's attachment to this story of a lost child. She knows very well I've been dig-ging around in the history of mother-and-baby homes and other institutions. She knows of the revelations about Tuam and Bessborough and the furore over the Commission of Investigation. My mother knows that the fact that a phalanx of grown-ups kept our cousin Mary's existence secret from us children, leaving her to grow up in the county home barely 25 miles from her real home, is eating away at us all. She chucks in a little grenade. Hah! she says, there's loads more you don't know about your grandmother, about what people went through.

And she is also saying, there's more you don't know about secrets, and how to keep them, and why and how people tell them. She is throwing down a challenge, from a world of intimate yet inchoate knowledge, in which stories are handed down in families as in a game of Chinese Whispers, to the supposedly verifiable knowledge held in the historical archive. Which kind of evidence do you trust? She knows I can't resist. I will burrow away in the archive to establish, as best I can, a set of parameters for what happened, even if I never get to the bottom of it. But there is another aspect to the challenge that has very little to do with 'what actually happened'.

My mother's stories are almost always about what was not said; they are little exercises in reading what's missing. In nearly all her tales she figures as an interpreter – of things stumbled on, intuited, unspoken. I learn from these stories about the culture of silence into which she was inducted, and about how information was withheld and knowledge circulated, particularly between women. I learn something about the forces that controlled rural society in late-nineteenth- and early-twentieth-century Ireland, especially when it came to sex, that made secret-keeping – or at the very least, silence – necessary. By keeping and selectively sharing secrets women conspired to retain some autonomy, even agency, in communities in which they often had little choice over what happened to them – where sex was highly regulated, under constant surveillance, and sometimes forced. And I think I may also be able to learn something about the disaster that occurred when those local, familial and intimate habits of secrecy and concealment met the modern institutions designed by the new Irish state to manage and contain them.

Something is encrypted in this strangely abstract fable about an illegitimate child, a child so insubstantial it's scarcely there at all. But what? My mother's storytelling is a gift to me, but it needs careful handling, like a poisoned apple. I need the apple, to have something to build my own story on, to begin to work out what happened before I was born. But I have to make sure I don't actually eat from it. I've learnt that caution from her, of course. Just look at the way she tells her parents' tales, with that little sceptical twist. She's not going to bite in, blithely, to her mother's apple. She keeps a careful distance. But as she speaks, I can feel her yearning to step over the threshold and join that cast of characters back in the land of childhood. Or in the grave, where her mother and her siblings lie, waiting for her to join them.

9.

My grandmother's fare to America was paid three times, or so the story goes. In 1909 or 1910, when she was seventeen or eighteen, the money was sent but no ticket was bought. The packet arrived again a few years later, and then, in the late 1910s, the fare was sent a third time. Her siblings, her aunts and her uncles were persistent. They sent news from South Boston, and from towns further up the coast where they found work and marriage partners and began families. Once her brother Timothy, who was older by nearly ten years, and had left for America in 1903 or 1904, returned for a visit. It was 1917 and he had been drafted into the United States Army so that he got to travel back to Europe for free. He spent his first leave back home in Ireland. He met his mother and his sister, all grown up now and working for a wage. He walked the lanes with her, tall in his uniform and good boots. And shortly after he went back to the Front he was killed.

West Cork, Wales, England, America, France: everyone was moving about. But until she was in her late sixties, and my parents were getting married in England, my grandmother never went further than Cork. The way the tale is told in our family is that her mother couldn't bear to be parted from her, her youngest child. Rather than working as a domestic servant in Boston, or in the glue factory in Peabody, Massachusetts, she lived in as a servant on a middling-sized farm managed by a widow and her three adult children, a few miles from home. And the money for her passage was spent by her family on something else instead.

I wonder what happened, after the first time? Why did her brothers and sisters send the money again? Did she write to them in secret, saying she'd manage it this time? And then, when the money was diverted once more – to cattle, or rent, or simply to pay the bill at the creamery – did she beg them a third time? Or was she the stubborn one? 'I'll not go, and you won't make me.' There is another story about Molly in her twenties that speaks to her obstinacy. It happened on a fair day. She went with her mother to town in the pony and trap, carrying the butter to sell in the market. Her mother had arranged with a matchmaker for her to meet a prospective husband, but when she looked through the window of the shop where they were to meet she saw his clay-caked hobnailed boots under the table. She must have seen his face too, but the story is about the boots. She turned and ran out of town, walking the 6 miles home.

'You'll never marry now!' said her mother when she caught up with her. Which is revealing, when you think about it. It suggests not only that there was no money at home, but also that there was no thought that the money from America could be saved towards a marriage. Apart from her youth and her health she had no assets. Molly's mother was a widow and she was a servant – she was being palmed off on an ineligible old farmer, with one pair of boots, and she knew it. When she turned and ran she must have known, too, that it was likely she would 'never marry now!' and she very nearly didn't.

My mother calls me on the phone to ask how the book is going, and I give a politely vague answer. She knows I'm writing it, but we both steer clear of what exactly I'm writing about. Women's lives in the past – that's about as specific as we get. She likes to tell me details of life on the farm in the 1930s: the pots with three legs and the ones that hung from a hook over the fire, and which kind of pot you used to bake bread or boil potatoes; her first day at school when she was given two pencils by her teacher, Mr Kiely; the day her older brothers used her as a marker in a game of bowls (played with stones) and her forehead was gashed open by an ill-aimed throw. At five or six she could be entrusted with collecting eggs from the hens, drawing water from the well, and driving the cows home from the long field. It wasn't hard. The cows knew better than she did how to manage things. She called out a few cowy words and they set amblingly off while she looked for blackberries in the hedge. When she let the ferrets out of their cages in the back kitchen they ran along her arms and across the back of her neck. They dived and leapt from the sacks of corn and wheat.

But the stories aren't always charming. When I asked her about the death of her brother Robert, this is what she remembered. Robert was nearly two years old when he died, in the fiercely cold January of 1938. My mother would have been seven and a half. The weather was so bad that year that the Travellers who usually camped at the bottom of the hill were camped at the top, because the fields were so deep in snow. My grandmother had nothing in which to bury her son, and one of the Traveller women took his christening robe and lengthened the sleeves with lace edging. Little loops and scallops. The women dressed him together, and my grandfather took him to town in the trap to be buried. My mother knew to say Traveller, but as she told the story she kept hesitating and almost using the word Tinker instead. I wanted to say, It's OK, call them what you want. They were part of your world.

More and more my mother's stories are about the relationship between her parents. How her father would take them blackberrying and place the fattest, juiciest berries on top for them to present proudly when they got home. 'Don't tell your mother!' How he would go out 'on a batter' and wouldn't be seen for days. When he got home from town, the worse for drink, he'd fling himself down on the settle and scatter coins from his pocket for the children. 'Don't tell your mother!' Once he drove the pony and trap so fast up the main street in Bally-dehob that people fled, screaming, and my distraught aunt Mary was convinced she would fall out. For my mother this story – told to her by her still white-knuckled sister when they got home – is evidence of her father's 'vulnerability'. I think she means his loneliness. I think of it as a kind of protest against the life that engulfed him.

'Don't tell!' – the recourse of all those who can't keep secrets. You keep them for me! My grandfather Tom was clearly hope-less when it came to not telling. Everything was on the surface. The drunkenness, the affection, the despair – he didn't know how to conceal any of it. But he married a woman with super-human secret-keeping abilities.

Take the case of one of my mother's older sisters, 'Mary that died'. Another death of a child, though not, like Robert, through illness in the dead of winter, but through carelessness. Every evening when the family knelt to say the rosary they included in their prayers 'Mary that died'. This was to differen-tiate her from Mary that lived, who was born a year after her sister's death and who took her name – and who was right there in the room, shifting about from knee to knee while they said their prayers. The first Mary's death at eighteen months old was sudden, and apparently unexplained. It wasn't until many years later, after my mother had left home for England, that she found out what really happened. This is not one of those stories that my mother has held close until the end of her

life. It has been part of our family history since I was young.
But originally it was a secret.

Early in their married life my grandparents lived with their
growing family in a labourer's cottage near Ballydehob, and
my grandmother's mother lived with them. Later my grandfather inherited some money from his much older brother Jack,
who was (as the story goes) killed in a fight in Marblehead,
Massachusetts – surely, I used to think, not a real place, but
manifestly I was wrong. They used the inheritance to buy
the farm where we spent our childhood summers. And they
splashed out. My mother remembers, in the mid-1930s when
she was five or six years old, a drive in an actual taxi – a car,
with a driver, not a pony and trap – to see distant relatives in
Drimoleague, everyone dressed in their finery. They were
enjoying their new wealth and they were certainly showing off.
Look at us now! But for the first twelve years of their marriage,
and through the birth of six children, including my mother, the
family squeezed into the cottage, grew vegetables on the small
patch of land, and my grandfather worked for local farmers.
Sometimes he took on seasonal jobs such as mending roads
for the county council. I know this from sources beyond my
family; I know it because occasionally he didn't mend the roads
he was contracted to mend, and the council brought him up
before the local magistrates, and fined him, with the case docu-
mented in court records.

Mary was born in September 1922 – at the height of the Civil
War, and a couple of weeks after Michael Collins was killed in
an ambush 30 miles away at Béal na Bláth. Half a million people
lined the roads for his funeral in Dublin at the end of August,
or so they said.

One day in May 1924, when her mother and grandmother
were distracted by tasks, or simply distracted, the child Mary

drowned in the well. When I first heard this story, I assumed it was a brick or stone well, something you'd have to climb up on in order to fall down into. The kind of well you find in a children's book. And since it was in the country, I imagined it covered in moss, with ferns growing out of the cracks between stones. But it wasn't like that. It was a shallow stream near the cottage, from which they drew water in a bucket. Mary must have toddled to the stream when their backs were turned, and when they found her it was too late.

The two women took the dead child, dressed her in dry clothes, and put her to bed. When my grandfather got home, they told him that she had suddenly become ill and died. I've looked up the death record (naturally), and the cause of death is registered as 'probably croup'. Then again, the record states that my grandfather was present at his daughter's death, which apparently he wasn't. I don't know where she is buried.

I have known this story for decades. It is the first dead baby story. It was not a secret my mother felt she needed to guard. I used to think the story was about the horror of discovery, and the fear – shared by both mother and grandmother – of what would happen if their responsibility for Mary's death became known. It was also a story about an alliance and an understanding between two women. Perhaps too it is a story about a strange form of kindness – would it have been better for my grandfather to know that his daughter had died through carelessness, rather than a sudden illness, or an unexplained medical condition? And it is certainly a story about extraordinary levels of reserve. Even amid the grief over the loss of the child, neither woman cracked. Was one of them more responsible than the other for the accident? Did one of them owe the other for their silence? At any rate my grandfather Tom never knew, not even after the death of Molly's mother.

When and why was the cover ever blown? At some point in the early 1950s, after her husband's death, Molly told her daughters the story of what had happened to their sister long before they were born. My mother was home from England for the summer. She and her sisters were sitting around the fire and talking, when my grandmother leant in to poke at the embers. She had her back to everyone when she suddenly blurted out, 'It was drowned in the well Mary was.' Nearly thirty years of painful secrecy was out, but at first no one could understand. As the story unfolded my grandmother told them not only that Mary had drowned, but that she and her mother had kept the secret – from everyone except the priest.

My grandmother shared the secret with her grown-up daughters and in doing so she handed over some of the responsibility, if not for what happened then for how it was remembered. Later, when we were old enough, my mother and my aunt shared the secret with their daughters. In each generation, men (apart from the priest who heard Confession) weren't involved. Secrets disappear in the moment of their telling, but they bind women together as responsible agents, as people who know.

And now, in turn, my mother tells me secrets: stories about her older sisters, Mary that died and Mary that lived, stories about her mother, and stories about Jackie and Lily and Stephen, knowing I may write them down. It is as though she is willing me to write them, but this is never explicitly said. She is feeding me information, but as long as we both stay quiet about what is going on, she can plausibly claim, to herself as much as to anyone else, that we are just chatting about the past. In reality, she wants the story told without the responsibility for telling it. She wants it said, without being the one who says it. We are both playing a game, but the rules have changed a lot over the years. When I first went to the Convent of Mercy in the 1990s to look at my cousin's records, I knew I could tell no one about my visit. In effect I created a new secret to add to the number of secrets and silences that were embedded in my family. Now, I'm being asked to tell. I'm being fed clues and bits of information, so that I'm no longer a spy so much as an accomplice.

But there is another level to the game, and another layer of secrecy. My mother believes that she is passing me information about her parents, and her siblings, and the world she lived in before she married my father. And this is partly true. But she is also passing me information about herself, and I am also writing about her. I don't believe that this has occurred to her, or not clearly. And I am not about to point it out.

IO.

Here is one of my mother's stories, handed down, or stolen, from her mother. It's about a man, in his fifties and then in his sixties, who used to pass by the farm in the 1930s and 1940s looking for a bed for the night, or a meal, in exchange for odd jobs. Later – when he was very old – the bed and the meal weren't exchanged for anything. His name was Arthur Murphy and often he slept in the hayloft above the chicken house. In bad weather he would sleep on the settle near the fire in the main room, under the pictures of the Holy Family, St Philomena, and the Sacred Heart with its tiny oil light underneath. Once, my mother got up early to take the bus and then the boat back to her nursing job in England – this would have been the early 1950s – and washed and dressed in the half-light in front of the fire, before she realized that Arthur Murphy was lying there, one eye squinting open.

Arthur was a 'school boy' – one of the many former pupils of the Baltimore Fisheries School, an industrial school for boys opened in the late 1880s to teach orphans and abandoned children skills in net-making, fish-curing and agricultural labour. The boys mostly moved on to an itinerant living on the farms round about. The home, which closed in 1950, had a dreadful reputation. Three or four of the school boys – they were never able to shake off their institutional upbringing, however old they were – were regular occupants of my grandmother's settle. One winter Arthur had outstayed his welcome. My grandmother Molly was trying to get him to move on, putting her case now this way and now that. 'Wouldn't you go up to the county home, Arthur, where it is warm and you'd be out of the weather?'; 'Wouldn't you think of the Home now, Arthur, where they'll give you a clean bed?' The county home was what used to be called the Workhouse or Poor House, one of the huge Victorian Poor Law institutions where the destitute and the old and the needy could get 'indoor relief'. The conditions in county homes in the 1940s weren't as bad as they had been when they were workhouses proper, but they were regimented places, where the food was awful, and the buildings themselves, which had not been improved for years, were cold, damp and comfortless. Arthur must have known the place well, as he knew the orphanage in Baltimore. Eventually he looked at her sideways and asked, 'If it's so good in the Home, why don't you go there so?'

My grandmother screeched with laughter whenever she told this story, and as my mother tells it now she's laughing too. He had put her in her place. Let's have no more pretending, he was saying, about relative comfort and care. She had her own home with a good fire, and she ought to share it. Arthur's back-answer became a family catchphrase, whenever any unpleasant task needed doing, from going to school to mucking out the byre in bad weather. 'If it's so good, why don't you go there so?'

What Arthur was pointing out was that the county home was there for my grandmother's good as much as Arthur's. It gave her a way out of having to help him. But perhaps there's more to it. I wonder whether her enjoyment of this story had partly to do with the fact that at one time she might, in fact, have gone to the county home herself. And maybe Arthur Murphy knew that.

*

I enjoy my mother's stories, but they are only going to get me so far. If I'm going to understand how Molly thought about things in the 1950s – and why she did what she did – I need to reach back beyond the things my mother can remember to Molly's childhood, much of which Molly couldn't remember either, and couldn't tell stories about because she was too young. I'm going to have to tack between family anecdotes and the bits and pieces I can put together from public records and history books. There's not a single family letter to give me any deeper insight into what anyone thought – or even where anyone was at any given moment. That is, not a single letter has been kept. I guess that the odd letter was written, to and from America, Wales, or England, announcing arrival times, births and deaths, or sending money. Even a few lines might tell me something. But although my grandparents were literate their parents were not. Apart from my mother's puzzling tales and a few family anecdotes, all I have to go on are a handful of photographs, census records and public registers. It's a meagre-enough haul, but it gives me a start.

Molly was born in October 1891, so her birth record says, the same week that Charles Stewart Parnell, the disgraced leader of the Irish Parliamentary Party, died in a house on the seafront in Brighton, at the age of forty-five. Accounts of his death like to include the detail that he passed into the next world 'in the arms' of Katherine O'Shea, the mother of his three children. Parnell had married O'Shea a few months earlier after a long, adulterous love affair and the scandal of a divorce (hers) that wrecked Irish nationalist hopes for a generation – indeed longer. How ironic that the seeds of my family's crisis around unmarried motherhood should have been laid in an Irish national crisis over sex, dishonour and marital respectability! The O'Shea divorce, which brought to light the alternative family set-up that Parnell and Kitty had arranged, pitted the Catholic Church in a struggle for power against nationalist politicians. Parnell had been at the height of his authority in the late 1880s, after ten years of successful strategizing over land reform and tenants' rights. Home Rule for Ireland looked like it was just around the corner. But since the Famine the Catholic Church had also been growing in institutional power. A 'devotional revolution' involving a huge church-building campaign, and a crusade to increase spiritual vocations and everyday religious practice, was near complete by the 1890s; Parnell's 'immorality' and the ensuing divorce case provided an opportunity for the clergy to assert the Church's supremacy in the political sphere, sidelining more radical, secular elements in the nationalist movement.

My guess is that the talk around the hearth of the thatched cabin into which my grandmother had so recently arrived was disputatious. Her eldest brother was twenty-one years older than she was. He was soon to leave home for labouring work in Wales, but in 1891 he was on the cusp of adulthood and greedy for change. Land reform and tenants' struggles for fair rents had shaped his teenage years. When he was ten years old a woman in the neighbouring parish of Schull had allegedly died of starvation following the series of poor harvests in the late 1870s. Her death caused a scandal, evoking memories of the Famine of the 1840s, and fuelling support among small tenant farmers for the radical politics of Parnell's Land League. The neighbouring towns of Ballydehob and Skibbereen were focal points for the land agitation in the early 1880s, with weekly meetings of local farmers that took on the character of unofficial courts of law. There were calls for landlords to be starved out themselves and refused rents. My great-grandfather was bringing up a growing family on about 10 acres of land

and he likely went to those meetings, taking his teenage sons with him.

But ten years later the tide had turned, as Ireland's bishops condemned Parnell for his immorality, and priests denounced Parnellites from the pulpit. Every day there was something in the paper about it. At card games and after Sunday Mass there was nothing but talk about it. Molly's brother took his father's side in support of Parnell against his pious mother, who, even if she didn't believe everything that was said about him by the priests and the bishops, was going to say she did. 'Right! Right! They were always right! God and morality and religion come first.' The Christmas dinner argument between those on the side of faith and those on the side of politics, described by James Joyce in his portrait of his Dublin childhood, was happening with minor variations by firesides and in kitchens up and down the country. Meanwhile my grandmother lay swaddled in the bottom drawer, blinking at the rafters.

She was the first baby in the house for nine years – or the first to survive. Her mother was in her late forties when she was born, and as the story went in our house, she gave birth to thirteen children, seven of whom made it through infancy. The tiny farm was far too small to support a family of that size, and the two-roomed cottage was impossibly crowded. Once they reached their early teens the children were hired out to live with local farmers, and their wages were paid directly to their father. On summer evenings and on Sundays they walked back home to see their mother, leaning in over the half-door and squinting through the turf smoke. Later, when their older siblings sent the prepaid tickets from America, they went to Queenstown to take the boat across the Atlantic.

Molly's sister Ellen was turning eighteen when Molly was born and she would soon be leaving for America. But for now she helped her mother, and got bits of work on nearby farms. Given the age difference, and the long gap before my grandmother was born, I can't help wondering whether the person who performed the role of Molly's mother to the outside world wasn't her mother at all. Was Molly instead the daughter of one of the girls she was to come to think of as her sisters, and who were now fussing around her: folding the blankets a little tighter, reaching out a hand to press warmth against her back to reassure her, crooking a finger for her to suck. Passing off a baby as the child of its grandmother or of an aunt was one of the most common ways of handling an unwanted pregnancy. Who reached down when she began to mewl, and brought her up to her breast? Whose chest ached with the weight of milk, and whose nipples were cracked and sore? Was it Ellen, who moved about red-faced and embarrassed in front of her father, so that it was hard to tell whether she felt penitent or defiant? My conjecture may be fanciful, but it is not outlandish. When I wondered aloud about it to my mother she didn't, as I expected, snort with laughter at the very idea. She said simply, 'Well, that wasn't something I ever heard.' That settles it, perhaps. One of the things this book is about is the strange way that people do hear things, even if they are never explicitly said.

However, it may not have settled it for my grandmother. Conceiving and giving birth to a healthy child when you are pushing fifty ('through the frost', as people said) isn't quite the miracle of Sarah in the Old Testament, but it is uncommon. Even if her mother lied to her about her age (and everybody in that community, men and women alike, seemed prone to shaving a few years off) I wonder that my grandmother didn't wonder. And if it crossed her mind that she might be someone else's child, I wonder what bearing that might have had on what happened later.

Not long ago I made a chance discovery that casts a new light on that race home from the matchmaker and the match. My mother asked me to get hold of a copy of her mother's birth certificate. She would like to see it, she said. I busied myself with the online Irish Registry of Births, Marriages and Deaths, and found my grandmother's birth recorded in October 1891. She was a couple of years older than she had ever let on to her children, who thought she was born in 1893. While I was at it, I searched for the record of her marriage to my grandfather, which I'd understood took place in 1919. Their first child was born in the autumn of 1920. But the record showed that my grandparents had actually married in June 1920, three months before John – my uncle Jackie – was born.

Six months is a very long time to wait, not knowing what you are going to do about the baby growing inside you. I can say this with some authority. But in a small community in West Cork in 1920, six months must have felt like an eternity. So I wonder about the order in which the fares were sent from America, the pregnancy, the match that was turned down, the marriage to my grandfather. When my grandmother turned and fled from the man with the clay-covered boots, was she already pregnant? Was this a match her mother had worked hard to pull off, to 'save her from shame'? For his part, the farmer would have acquired an heir as well as a woman to slave for him. That cry, 'You'll never marry now!', may not simply have been the impatient cry of a mother annoyed that her plans had gone awry, but real anguish over the future that lay ahead of her daughter. Did this look like a last chance? In which case my obstinate grandmother was very, very lucky.

What do you do when you discover something you're not supposed to know? It was just so easy to type the names and dates into the registry's search engine. Once upon a time I'd have had to travel to Dublin and queue at a desk in the research room of the General Register Office in Werburgh Street, or fish for land registry documents at the 1970s curvy-concrete-and-glass Irish Life Centre, or line up with the Americans on holiday checking out the genealogical services available at the National Library of Ireland on Kildare Street. I know because I've done all these things. All the queuing and form-filling and waiting about offers some kind of ballast to the information that is eventually handed over. You've worked hard for it. Now you just click on 'Image' and there it is, the 1920s handwriting, the marriage of labourer and servant, the witnesses' names that meant nothing to me, the date.

I was puzzled by the record I'd found, and even – though it was there in black and white – disbelieving. The idea of my rather puritanical and upright grandmother consenting to sex before marriage was too outlandish to credit, although it was of course possible she had not consented. But when I tentatively broached the subject with my mother, I found that the pre-marital pregnancy was not, as I had assumed, a secret. Or not a very well-kept one.

'I've found something strange . . . ,' I began, but before I could get to the end of my explanation my mother interrupted me. Yes, she said, she knew all about that. She had worked it out when she was fifteen or sixteen, soon after her father died, when reminiscing around the fire had turned to her parents' wedding in the summer of 1920. Another fireside revelation, but an unintended one. My mother had done the maths, but apart from one pointed question to her mother – 'What did you wear to get married?' (the answer was a blue suit, which, figured my teenage mother, might have hidden the bump pretty well) – she kept it to herself. She had said nothing more to her mother or any of her siblings, either then, or in the seventy-plus years that had since passed. But she had certainly not forgotten. She had filed it away, and I didn't even need to get to the end of my sentence before she knew exactly what I was talking about.

It struck me then that it was quite possible her siblings had done the maths too, either on that same January evening or at any other time when their parents' wedding was recalled. It was quite possible that there had been numerous occasions when this information was made available in conversation, but for the pieces to be added together some additional element – some background awareness, some curiosity – had to be added to the mix. I think of my mother's sudden understanding as a kind of bodily knowledge. Her own body was readying itself for sex and pregnancy (blood, breasts, moods, desires) and information that had meant nothing to her at the age of ten or eleven could now be processed. But it could not be acknowledged. My mother knew this wasn't something to talk about, even to her sisters.

My mother kept it to herself, but I did the opposite. I didn't want to know on my own. I rang my sisters and cousins in turn and told them what I'd discovered. And now I'm telling you. You'd be forgiven for wondering why. Surely my grandmother's sexual history is of interest only to me and to the people who knew her. Yet here I am, writing about it. For months I've done little else but write about it.

I follow the clues my mother lays down like a child being led to a gingerbread house. It looks so good to eat but inside there is something lurking. I don't think my mother is a witch, but she may have me under her spell. I listen to her stories; I check the records; I feed it all back to her. I think back to the moment when I looked at my grandparents' marriage certificate and understood what it meant, and I realize that what I caught in my mother's lightning-quick response to the news – yes, she knew all that – was relief. I was finally catching up.

Silences are not the same as secrets. My grandmother's pre-marital pregnancy was not unknown to those around her, it was just unspoken. You might say that my mother respected her parents' privacy, but perhaps it was less generous than that. She was burdened by knowledge she felt she could not share, or could not quite bear – her mother as a sexual person, a desiring woman. In effect she entered into a kind of silent complicity with her mother without her mother ever knowing.

But now she wants to tell. There is no real human cost to the telling. It is not as though there is anything left to be complicit in. Not only is there no one still alive to be harmed, but the fact of sex before marriage is hardly dangerous information these days. Nothing rests on keeping silent except the fact of silence itself. But I can't help feeling that my long-dead grandmother is just a little bit less safe now.

My Grandmother's Secrets

II.

Molly must have realized that she was pregnant sometime in the spring of 1920. She was twenty-eight years old. Her breasts grew sore, and her bowels didn't seem at all right. She tossed and turned at night, but she kept her counsel. Later, when her period didn't come, and still didn't come, she spoke to her lover. Had it been a one-off fumble in a barn after a dance? Fingers tugging at buttons, hands searching under layers. A bit of sport that went too far and was afterwards regretted? Or were they dedicated lovers, who stole opportunities to meet in secret? Did he tell her that what they were doing was safe, that he would pull out in time? Were they known to be courting? If I try to imagine the scene I get stuck inside the conventions of an Edwardian costume drama set among the rural poor – the film of a lost late work by Thomas Hardy about life lived somewhere between Dorset and the West of Ireland, complete with milking stools. They walk the lanes in summertime after the long day's tasks are over; he watches her when she brings the gallon can of tea across to the men stooking hay, or footing turf; he happens on her picking blackberries and pulls down the arching canes so she can reach; they sit together at card games or dances; they meet after dark.

It is of course most likely that the man she married six months later was the father of her child, although it is not an absolute given. Perhaps she was pregnant by someone else who upped and left. Perhaps the pregnancy was the result of rape. She wouldn't be the first young woman to try to find a man to step in to look after her, and she won't be the last. Perhaps she grew tired of waiting for him to declare himself, and the sex was a calculated gamble. Demographers and historians of illegitimacy argue that early in the nineteenth century, and in the first couple of decades after the Famine, getting pregnant before marriage was one of the few ways open to women of securing their future. It was a risky business, to be sure, but if the couple were already promised to one another, she could rely on relatives and the community around her to make sure the marriage took place. But I doubt my grandmother took such a calculated risk in 1920. By then the newly revamped post-Famine Catholic Church had consolidated its campaign to control sexual habits, in the name of Irish purity, and sexual lapses were not accepted or understood with anything like the same spirit as fifty years earlier. She must have had a fair idea of the mountain of trouble she would face if she got pregnant. In the yearly parish missions, and sometimes on ordinary Sundays, priests thundered out their sermons on the sins of the flesh, leaving listeners in no doubt of the degradation they'd be calling down on their family as well as themselves should they commit the sin of fornication.

Most likely it was furtive sex – clothed, and in the dark – that 'went too far'. Her lover might have offered her reassurance that he'd be careful, or that if the worst happened, they'd get married, but I guess that the idea of consent as we understand it today hardly came into it. Even in the 1950s and 1960s advice columns in women's magazines were warning girls that they were prey to men's uncontrollable urges, and a respectable girl or woman was not supposed to make the mistake of giving those urges a chance. One thing is clear: the baby was born in early September, so this wasn't a midsummer dalliance. Sometime over Christmas 1919 or New Year 1920 she let her guard down, maybe once or maybe many times, and now she was in trouble. Her lover did not immediately step in to save her.

She had no father to intervene; no brothers who would defend her honour. The family home had long since broken up, after the death of her father when Molly was ten. Most of her siblings were in America. The small cottage where she had been born was slowly falling to ruin and by 1911 it had only one serviceable room, where her brother, recently returned from Wales, lived with his new wife and small baby. Since her late teens Molly had been living-in as a servant on a farm about 5 miles away in Glannakilleenagh – a walk across fields of a little more than an hour. The farmhouse was a solid, two-storey building on around 60 acres of land, with stables, two cow-houses, a pigsty, a dairy, barns, a store for potatoes and a shop. Her mistress, Bridget Goggin, was a widow in her late seventies, and Molly lived and worked alongside the widow's children: a daughter and two sons, all older than her by ten to fifteen years.

I can glean this much from the census records, but the tiny entries don't help much in trying to imagine how it felt to live this life. All I can say with any certainty is that she lived in considerably greater physical comfort with the Goggins than if she had stayed at home – in a large house, on a farm that was prosperous enough to support a small shop. I don't know if she was still there when she fell pregnant. My guess is that she was not. In February 1914 Bridget's daughter married, in the church at Kilcoe, and left the farm. The following winter Bridget died, of pneumonia and heart disease. This would have left my grandmother alone on the farm with two brothers in their late thirties, unless one or both of them had volunteered for the war. Either way it was no place for a woman on her own.

Perhaps Molly went to live with her mother Mary in the

rented cottage in Cappagh Beg, or Lissaclarig, or Hollyhill. Every few years, after her husband died, Molly's mother moved a few miles to a new cabin or cottage where she had to start again with a little bit of garden, and some chickens. I've found her in at least four different townlands in the 1910s. She was in her seventies, and when I first saw evidence of all the shifting about, I interpreted it as a sign of the precariousness of her life in old age. She could neither read nor write; she had been squeezed off the smallholding to make room for her son's family and she wasn't exactly getting to take her ease. But I think now that that is a misreading. From 1909, people who had reached the age of seventy (or who could persuade an official that they had reached that age) could claim a pension of 5 shillings a week, under the Old Age Pensions Act of 1908. For my great-grandmother, who turned seventy around 1913 or 1914, 5 shillings was a substantial sum, and a good deal more than she had lived on for long periods of her life before that. In her old age she became 'well off' and could choose where and with whom she lived, because she now had an income. All the moving about was a sign of her purchasing power. Later she went to live with my grandparents, and no doubt they were glad of the money she brought with her. In the end my great-grandmother lived into her nineties, well beyond the frost and into deep midwinter. My mother remembers her as an old woman. For the first five years of her life my mother lived with a woman whose own first years had been lived during the worst of the Famine.

Still, it is unlikely that Molly went to live with her mother in her mid-twenties, because she needed to bring money in, and the only available work for a young woman with her background was as a farm servant. I imagine she went to 'live-in' on another farm, and indeed on her marriage certificate in 1920 she lists her occupation as 'servant'. And perhaps her pregnancy was one result of that choice. Living in close quarters with strangers, lacking the protection of fathers and brothers, servants were vulnerable. Illegitimacy rates were low in Ireland, by international standards – and part of the reason for this was that there were relatively few domestic servants. Rural Ireland was simply not prosperous enough to support a large class of live-in servants – most people employed on small and middling-sized farms were relatives of the farmer rather than paid help (although it is true that being a relative is no guarantee of protection from sexual violence or harassment).

The fact that my grandmother was working as a live-in servant was one of the ways she was Victorian – even in the 1910s. She was a member of a dying breed. Throughout the late nineteenth century the numbers of agricultural labourers and servants – hired workers who didn't own their own land or property – plummeted in Ireland. At the turn of the century more than two-thirds of farm workers in England were hired labourers; in Ireland it was barely 18 per cent. Why the difference? It was one of the knock-on effects of the Famine. Landless labourers and servants had been hardest hit by the potato blight. They had few resources to fall back on and they had died (or, if they were lucky, had managed to emigrate) in far greater numbers than tenants who held land. And for those who survived, the economies of the farm meant that families increasingly employed their own relatives, rather than hired help – relatives destined to remain single, who were expected to remain chaste and celibate.

The change didn't happen overnight. My grandmother's much older brothers and sisters had probably hired themselves out as young teenagers in the 1880s, in order to contribute back home and earn their passage money to the United States.

It was something you did for a few years while you saved for your fare, or for a dowry. But by the time my grandmother reached her teens working as a hired servant in a stranger's home was more unusual – it was for the most economically insecure. I wonder how she felt about it. I wonder how much she minded that she had no security and no financial support. My guess is that she minded a lot. I think of the way she became so attached to her farm years later, when I was a child, so immovable even. The farm was her reward, long dreamt of, and she had no intention of being displaced, least of all, in 1954, by her feckless son's lover.

After all, she could have left for America in her teens, as most of her siblings had done. For those, like my grandmother, living right at the precarious edge of economic survival, domestic service in the United States was a far safer investment in the future. But Molly stayed in Ireland, and in the spring of 1920 she was in a fix.

12.

When I set out to try to work out how my grandmother lived with the knowledge that her son's lover and her child (her own granddaughter) were confined to the county home, excluded from the family, the very last thing I expected to discover was that my grandmother had been in exactly the same boat thirty-five years previously. The very last thing I thought I'd find out was that my grandfather had got his much younger neighbour pregnant in 1920, with the child who was later going to repeat the sins of his father and get his much younger neighbour pregnant in turn. I had thought that I was investigating a culture of excessive piety, which placed a premium on respectability and moral prudence, and that somewhere inside that nexus of Catholic, rural, land-hungry conservatism I would find the explanation for my grandmother's behaviour.

After all, I could remember her – the way she would get us all kneeling for the Rosary every night, the holy pictures, the strict adherence to a gendered division of labour. We girls were to learn to cook and to clean and to behave with modesty and to defer to boys, who would always come first. Once my sister Bridget – four years older than me and with a highly tuned sense of natural justice – got into a speechless rage when we all (sisters and cousins, girls and boys) came in exhausted from a back-breaking day picking potatoes and my grandmother insisted she pour the boys their tea and allow them to eat first. My mother laughed but didn't intervene.

But rather than a unique enclave of sexual reserve, the world

99

I was learning about was just as steeped in illicit sexuality as any other. And now, I think, why not? Irish men and women were not differently made from men and women elsewhere. There were illicit liaisons between couples, there was sex between men and between women, there were men, as there are men everywhere, who wouldn't take no for an answer. There was incest, and, especially behind the walls of the institutions, sexual abuse of children on a large scale. Irish people weren't more sexually continent than any other people, though they were, perhaps, better at covering it up in all sorts of informal ways: babies brought up by relatives or neighbours, couples emigrating, same-sex intimacies unspoken. Somehow, knowing all this, I was still surprised.

It seemed impossible to think of my grandmother as a sexual person. Or rather, it never occurred to me to do so. She was, admittedly, always on the look-out for foul play. She did not like it when I played alone with one of my boy cousins. She would rap on the ceiling with a broom handle and summon us down to the kitchen, or call up the field for us to stop whatever we were doing. Which was never anything, except the boys trying to impress their English cousins with their knowledge of cars or telling overheard stories about spies and the old IRA. At the time, as a girl of twelve or thirteen, I didn't understand my grandmother's concern. I was irritated by her hovering. Looking back now I can interpret her anxiety as rooted not so much in sexual puritanism as sexual awareness. Sex was everywhere, always waiting to waylay you, and you had to be permanently on guard.

My first thought when I realized that my grandmother was already pregnant when she married in 1920 was: what hypocrisy. I was full of righteous indignation over her rejection of her son's lover all those years later. Why couldn't you have helped that young woman? I wanted to ask. Lily was just a teenager. My grandmother knew what it felt like to be on the edge of being an outcast. She knew how vital it was to cover up the damage to her respectability. She knew that if she didn't marry, she was lost – and so was her child. Most of all, Molly knew that whatever her notions of 'stock' or social class, when it came to sexual morality she was no better than her son's lover. But perhaps she believed that no one else knew, or that they had forgotten. Perhaps she worked hard to forget it herself.

My sisters and cousins mostly responded in the same way – with expletive-strewn disbelief. But my cousin Caroline was more thoughtful, or maybe just more kind. When I told her about the six-month wait for the wedding in 1920 there was a short silence and then she said, 'She must have been so frightened.' And it's true. She must have been out of her mind.

It was, to put it mildly, terribly bad timing. She must have realized she was pregnant in February or March 1920, right in the middle of the Irish War of Independence – the guerrilla war fought between the IRA and forces of the British Crown between January 1919 and the ceasefire in July 1921. Most of the fighting took place in the urban centres of Belfast, Dublin and Cork, but there were very high levels of violence in rural Cork, including (on the Republican side) ambushing British army patrols, attacking police barracks, raiding for arms, and killing suspected spies and informers. And, on the British side, declaring martial law, executing Republicans, and burning and sacking towns. More than 530 people were killed in the county in the course of the war, over a third of them civilians. Molly discovered she was pregnant just at the point when authority was breaking down across the country. By early April 1920 the police force had effectively disappeared from rural areas, and

400 barracks had been burnt out, along with tax offices and other official buildings. Trains weren't running because transport workers were on strike. The justice system collapsed because jurors couldn't be got. There were two rival local governments battling over control of justice, law and order and social welfare. Molly's problem couldn't have been solved by police or jurors, but the general chaos cannot have made finding a solution any easier. After Mass at the newly built church, with its fancy stained-glass windows, on the new road from Skibbereen to Ballydehob, the latest events in the war were gone over. Who was there and who saw what and what were people saying? Molly pulled her winter coat around her, and tried to outstare the neighbours' appraising looks. Something had to be done, but what?

In truth she had few options. I can't know whether she used herbs like pennyroyal to try to bring on bleeding, whether she pressed her stomach against rocks, whether she tried jumping from a height or washing herself out with carbolic soap. Until the 1870s aborting a pregnancy before the foetus had quickened was a grey, or greyish, area in the Catholic hierarchy of sins – and anyway the rural Irish population was renowned for its lax religious habits, for ignoring or evading devotional practices, and for mixing them with folkloric customs. Curtseying to the fairies would as likely keep you safe from harm as attending weekly Mass. (I'm exaggerating, but not much.)

In the years immediately after the Famine only about a third of Catholics went to Mass or Holy Communion. There weren't enough priests and there weren't enough churches to serve the population, but there also wasn't enough money. The costs of marriage licences, burials, Masses for the dead, were prohibitive for the poor, even though there was a sliding scale that differentiated between shopkeepers and farmers, on the one hand, and labourers on the other. But the loss of 2 million people to death and emigration between 1846 and 1850 re-calibrated the ratio of priests (and nuns) to people. And because it was the respectable classes (shopkeepers and farmers) who had managed to survive the Famine more or less intact, the new reforming cardinal and bishops found themselves at an advantage. The labourers, cottiers and paupers, who had always been less rigorous in their support of the priests, were swept away. This made it all the easier for the reformers who were determined to clean up Irish Catholicism and extend their influence.

By the turn of the century, when Molly was going to school, the Irish were routinely described (especially by their own prelates) as the best Catholics in the world. A massive church-building campaign, a drive for weekly Mass attendance, parish missions, and the basic rule that sacraments such as baptisms, marriages and funerals should happen in church rather than at home – and within a couple of generations the power of the institutional Church was secure. The rosary, novenas, devotion to the Sacred Heart and the Immaculate Concep-tion, candles, vestments, incense, beads, scapulars, medals, missals: all the paraphernalia that we associate with old-timey Irish Catholicism was introduced in the 1860s and 1870s, as a way of capturing the imagination of the people – and policing their behaviour. As the Church spread its creeping influence over a newly thinned-out post-Famine landscape, it gained control over aspects of everyday life that people would once have regulated for themselves. 'Invalid marriages', informal family relationships, and mixed (Catholic–Protestant) mar-riages became a thing of the past. Parnell's relationship with Kitty O'Shea was just the most high-profile instance of collat-eral damage.

Over 90 per cent of Catholics had submitted to the new regime by the turn of the century – attending weekly Mass, confessing their sins, marrying and baptizing their children in church. The institutionalization of Catholicism laid the groundwork for the new Irish state not only in terms of Irish identity (being Catholic was increasingly synonymous with being Irish) but through its bureaucracy. The Church hierarchy liked to believe that Irish Catholics had become better behaved (less drunk, less violent, less ignorant, less subject to a culture of poverty) and more 'respectable' – better educated, more regulated – just at the point when arguments for Irish independence were at their height. The new power of the Catholic Church was one of the ways Irish culture was becoming modern. It was a story of triumph, but it was predicated on loss. There were, proportionally, more priests, doctors, police and officials of all kinds in post-Famine Ireland, but mainly because there were fewer people overall.

Irish Catholicism wasn't, for the most part, an intellectual religion. It catered for the spiritual needs of an agrarian society, promoting anti-urban values linked with everyday life and a rural economy: the community over the individual, frugality over profligacy, celibacy over sexual freedom, modesty over pride and independence. It should be no surprise that small farmers (and servants and labourers who aspired to be farmers, like my grandparents) identified so strongly with these values. They were the values of good husbandry, caution, conservatism; it was a set of beliefs that firmly put the family, and the family business of land ownership, first above all.

Illegitimacy, and the sexual activity to which it bore witness, was always a social problem, particularly so when families had money, property and respectability to lose. Women have always had to guard their sexual honour, but mainly because in losing it they rendered themselves 'spoiled goods', ineligible for marriage. Primogeniture and the laws of property inheritance only work when you can be sure – or as sure as possible – that the line of inheritance is a legitimate one. But the Irish Church's obsession with sexual purity (sexual modesty in women and celibacy before marriage) gave complete religious, institutional backing to private concerns about legitimacy. In the end this unholy alliance, between a puritanical, sex-obsessed Church and a land-obsessed, agrarian economy, almost strangled the Irish family out of existence.

My grandmother fell pregnant at a moment when sex outside marriage was becoming more strictly codified as a sin, for which women must atone in a penitentiary regime. The very fact that the nascent state opted for new mother-and-baby homes and other institutions was an acknowledgement that the system they had been relying upon to regulate the sexual lives of young people wasn't working well enough – and this despite the fact that illegitimacy rates in Catholic rural Ireland were low. What the clerical upholders of the new state wanted was to fashion a society that would become a model for the world, by controlling sexual activity – indeed by controlling pleasure – that did not enjoy official endorsement. And at the same time to save babies for God.

Molly's trouble came too early for the Bessborough Mother and Baby Home. Before 1922, if a woman's family wouldn't or couldn't help, her only hope was the workhouse, fleeing to England, or a Protestant home in Dublin. Elements within the Catholic Church were determined to do something about that. In 1921 the *Irish Ecclesiastical Record* published a series of essays drawing attention to the problem of proselytizing Protestant organizations that were offering help to unmarried mothers in exchange for their babies, who would be sent to Protestant homes. The charities were condemned as a form of 'souperism', the practice in Famine times of offering food in exchange for religious conversion. 'Girls from every county flock to Dublin' where Protestant homes were acting as 'agencies of perversion'. Since girls 'in trouble' will 'go anywhere to avoid publicity', Catholic organizations should 'copy the tactics of their enemies' and set up homes of their own.

In fact, most unmarried pregnant Catholic women in early twentieth-century Ireland didn't deliver their babies up to the Protestant homes in Dublin but gave birth in the workhouse – although not necessarily the one closest to home. Many women travelled to Dublin, or Liverpool, or London, in search of anonymity. The Report of the Commission on Mother and Baby Homes notes that:

> In 1905 there were 2,129 unmarried mothers and 2,764 children who were either 'illegitimate' or deserted in Irish workhouses. There were 2,783 unmarried mothers in English workhouses in 1920. Given that the population of England was nine times the population of Ireland, the figures indicate that a much higher proportion of Irish single mothers ended up in a workhouse, or, alternatively they remained there for a much longer period.

Molly must have considered the prospect of the workhouse, if only as a fate she was determined to avoid. ('Why don't you go there so?') But one of the first actions of the new Republican government in early 1919 was to dismantle the hated Poor Law and workhouse system. In each county one workhouse was to be designated as a hospital, another a county home for the destitute and infirm; others were to be closed once the Republicans had gained control of them, but that took time. The workhouses in Schull and Skibbereen were repurposed as garrisons for the beleaguered British forces and, as 'official' state institutions, they were magnets for raids and counterraids during the War of Independence. A grim prospect at any time, the workhouse was an impossible option in 1920.

And in the end, for Molly, it didn't come to that. There was, I think, a crisis in the spring of 1920 over whether her lover would or could marry her, and the search for an alternative match with the old farmer in his boots is one sign of this. Perhaps my grandfather was reluctant for all the old reasons; or perhaps it was a question of money. By the time Molly fell pregnant her father was long dead and her eldest brother was settled on the family holding with a growing family. He would have had, I'm guessing, no intention of providing funds for his feckless sister who had gone and got herself in trouble, even if he had had money to spare, which he hadn't. I can't help wondering whether the third package that came from Boston wasn't spent on her passage because she needed it for her marriage instead.

13.

The delay may have been about money, but neither of my maternal grandparents were in the dowry class. Dowries were a way of sharing out property and goods to siblings who weren't going to inherit the farm, but neither family had land or backing. My grandfather, Tom, was an agricultural labourer – his parents had both died long before, and he had no siblings to pay off, and indeed no settled home to bring his new wife into.

And there was a more obvious reason for the six-month delay. Tom, who was fifteen years older than Molly – forty-three, when they married – was a Protestant. A mixed marriage was no easy thing to pull off, and securing the consent of the local clergy may well have delayed the wedding. Molly was a god-fearing Catholic and a good parishioner. In order to marry in the Church – in order for them to live as part of the Catholic community – her future husband would have to 'turn'. Or rather, he was given to understand that he had to: to take official instruction in the Catholic faith and abjure his past religion. The Catholic Church was not going to risk the loss of my grandmother's baby to Protestantism, even if it meant no marriage. The objections to Protestant mother-and-baby homes as 'agencies of perversion' is one sign of that.

Only a generation earlier the mixed marriage would have seemed unremarkable. In fact, Tom was himself the product of a mixed marriage. His Protestant father, also a farm labourer, had married a Catholic woman in 1860. Two of his aunts lived in rented cottages in the same small townland, one married to a Catholic, the other to a Protestant. These were men and women of no property, landless labourers and servants. In 1851 my grandfather's relatives Thomas and James (one most likely Tom's uncle, and one his grandfather) were both bringing up families close to one another a few miles from Skibbereen, in houses valued at a rent of 5 shillings a year. Five shillings was the lowest possible rental valuation; below that and you didn't count, and in fact below that you probably hadn't survived the Famine. Many of the houses around them were abandoned: their destitute inhabitants had died of starvation and disease, or been evicted, or had somehow managed to get away. The 5-shilling holding offered no security. Twenty-five years later, in 1877 (the year Tom was born), a relative called Betty, who was the widow of either Thomas or James and so may have been Tom's grandmother (my great-great-grandmother), died in Skibbereen workhouse of 'old age'. She was seventy-one and her occupation is listed on the death record as 'mendicant'.

Landless Protestants in nineteenth-century Ireland are rarely talked about, in comparison with the stereotypical Protestant landowner, or substantial tenant farmer. But although they were likely to work for Protestant farmers and to sit behind them in the back pews at church, my grandfather's family had far more in common with landless Catholics than with their co-religionists who held land as tenants, never mind Protestant landowners. And they were far more likely to find a partner among the Catholic servant classes than to persuade a Protestant farmer's son or daughter to marry them.

A string of children born in my grandfather's extended family in the 1860s and 1870s emigrated to the Boston area in the 1880s and early 1890s, when they reached their late teens. Some of them worked in the glue factory in Peabody, where

Irish people from Lisheen and Ballydehob and Schull rendered down gelatine from the hooves and bones of cattle, sheep and horses – cast-offs from the tannery next door – by mixing them with lime and acid in large vats. When I visited the site recently, to get a sense of the landscape that my relatives had swapped for their small fields in the 1880s and 1890s, I was amazed to discover that the factory is still there, still rendering down collagen, but for beauty products now, not adhesive. Still there too is the eighteenth-century house – now a museum – that was used as dormitory accommodation for the Irish workers. The conditions must have been hellish, and the death records for Peabody in the 1890s repeatedly list the deaths from consumption of young Irish leather workers ('Morocco Dressers') and glue workers.

At least three, and maybe four, of my grandfather's older siblings worked in the Peabody glue factory, alongside their cousins and neighbours from home. There was Tom's brother James, who was born in the early 1860s and emigrated to Peabody in the mid-1880s. He married a girl from Ballydehob who also worked making glue, but a few years later he got sick and they came back to Ireland. He died of TB at home in his twenties. There was Jack, born in 1867, who followed his brother James a few years later and eventually got out of the factory and made a good living running a livery stable. (Presumably the old horses went to the tannery and were eventually made into glue.) By the end of his life he was working as a contractor in trucking, so he knew how to move with the times. He was living in the centre of the village of Marblehead, now a fancy dormitory town by the sea, and when he died in 1931 it was his bequest that enabled my grandparents to buy a farm.

And there was Sarah. Born in 1874, she was three years older than my grandfather Tom. Jack had left Ireland in the late

1880s, but in 1893 he came home for a visit and returned to Peabody with Sarah. She went into the glue factory like everyone
else. But she crops up again in the record two years later, when
she marries her first cousin (who had left Bantry ten years
earlier) in February 1895. Three months after the wedding a
daughter was born. I'm intrigued by this foreshadowing of my
grandparents' situation. Tom's much older cousin got Tom's
sister Sarah pregnant, and eventually married her six months
gone (or possibly he didn't get her pregnant but stepped in to

save her), just as Tom would eventually marry Molly, six months gone. Any thought that it would be easier for Sarah to face down a pre-marital pregnancy in Peabody in 1895 than for Molly in Ballydehob in 1920 should be resisted. Perhaps there was less talk to contend with. There were no parents to get round, and no one to tell them what to do, or what not to do. But there were other difficulties. By October 1895 both Sarah and her child were dead – the baby from cholera and my great-aunt from consumption.

As the youngest son, through all this Tom stayed home in Ireland, supporting his mother and one of his brothers, who contracted Parkinson's disease when he was young and never married. In 1911 the three of them were still living in a two-roomed stone cottage they rented from a Protestant farmer, Robert Talbot Beamish, in the townland of Ballybane, north of Ballydehob. Tom's relatives had been servants to the Beamishes, but servants who were intimate with the family. Tom's father John had been employed as a dairyman on Beamish's 100-acre farm. My great-grandmother assisted at the birth of the Beamishes' eldest son and heir, Thomas John, in 1895. For at least twenty years after his father died, Tom carried on working for the Beamishes and took on seasonal jobs for other farmers. From his house in Ballybane on a Sunday morning his mother went to Catholic Mass in the chapel, while he and his brother Stephen attended divine service in the Church of Ireland church.

For my great-grandparents in 1860 there had been no social pressure to marry within the tribe. It was immaterial who they chose to have children with, and there were no hard-and-fast rules about how the children in a mixed marriage would be brought up. Usually the father got to decide the religion of his children, and that was why my grandfather went to a

Protestant church and a Protestant school, while his mother curtsied to the priests and crossed herself and said the Rosary. But things were tightening up. In 1907 Pope Pius X issued the *Ne Temere* decree, which sharpened the rules around marriage for practising Catholics. From then on you had to be married by your own parish priest, or get a special dispensation to go somewhere else; you had to have the marriage registered; and even if you divorced in a civil court, if you were a Catholic you were still married in the eyes of the Church – you couldn't marry again. But the regulation that was to cause the most trouble (and several court cases) in Ireland was the one that stated that mixed marriages were only valid if the non-Catholic partner promised (in writing) that all children would be raised Catholic. The fear of proselytism, of losing children's souls to the other side, wasn't only focused on babies born in institutional homes, but children born in family homes as well. My grandparents could technically have married with this written promise about how the children would be brought up. But the parish priest and the local bishop wanted Tom to convert, and probably so did Molly.

'How did you believe it, Tom?' asked a Protestant neighbour years later, of my grandfather's conversion. You can hear the disdain even at this distance. And it would be unrealistic to think that all the efforts being made by the Catholic Church to position itself as the true heart of the Irish nation, and all the talk about the evils of Protestantism, and all the political rhetoric over the struggle for independence from the British Empire weren't having an effect on day-to-day relationships between Protestant and Catholic neighbours. Everyone was apparently on civil terms – nods on the road, polite trading in the shops, offers of help at harvest time and, I'm sure, genuine friendships. How else could my grandparents have got together? But there was no getting past the fact that the two communities were distinct. For my grandfather's neighbour it was impossible to imagine believing as a Catholic believed. There was surely pressure on him from the dwindling band of Protestant neighbours not to 'turn', and bargaining over the terms under which he should surrender to the priest.

But he did surrender, and by June 1920 my grandparents were married in the Catholic church at Kilcoe. I've spent some time staring at their marriage certificate online, to see if it can tell me anything. At the time they were living a few miles from one another across the fields. Tom gives his occupation as Labourer and his place of residence as Lisheenacrehig. Sometime after 1911, perhaps around the time of the First World War, my grandfather must have moved out of the cottage in Ballybane that was owned by the Beamishes. Maybe it had become uninhabitable. Or maybe after his mother died in the early 1910s the Beamishes had reclaimed the house. At any rate, by 1920 he was living a few miles further east, and closer to the Beamishes' main farm. And in addition to working for the Beamishes he was likely employed by the other Protestant farming families in the area, the Dalys, the Trinders, the Shannons, or the Swantons.

My grandmother gives her occupation on the marriage register as Servant, and her place of residence as Lissaclarig – a townland neighbouring Lisheenacrehig, near Ballydehob. I can't know for sure which family she was working for. There were nine families living in Lissaclarig East and West in 1911, and at least four or five of them occupied large enough farms to require the help of a farm servant. But by an extraordinary chance I recently happened to meet someone who gave me a lead. He was one of the directors of the Museum of London, Finbarr Whooley, and our meeting was about museum business, but chatting at the end I mentioned the search for my grandmother's whereabouts in the 1910s. He turned out to be from Lissaclarig, and – I still find this uncanny – he remembered his aunt saying that my grandmother used to work in his grandmother's kitchen. He was initially embarrassed to tell me that the reason he remembered such an unlikely detail was that his aunt liked to put on airs.

One of the ways she could prove that her family was of some importance was by reminding her nephews and nieces that Molly – now a respectable farmer whom they would see at Mass on Sundays – used to do their washing. The children turned it into a family joke against their snobbish aunt. But I wonder too whether Finbarr's aunt, who would have been nine in 1920, dimly remembered some part of a story about a baby that suggested that Molly hadn't always been as respectable as she seemed. At any rate this aunt could recall Molly preparing food for the family and helping out with other chores, fetching water, doing the washing. Doing the kind of work that I remember so well her doing in her own house in the 1960s and 1970s. It struck me then that Molly may have looked after Finbarr's father, when he was a baby. As we sat across the white melamine office table from one another the strange intimacy of this coincidence tracked across both our faces.

I don't know whether Molly lived-in with Finbarr's relatives or with another family, or perhaps rented a small cottage with her mother. (The 1911 census lists an empty house in Lissaclarig and perhaps that was where they lived, after it had been made habitable.) But I do know that by 11 September 1920, when Jackie was born, Molly and Tom were both living in Lissaclarig. The townland is listed on his birth record. Tom moved in with Molly after they married, not the other way round, and it is likely that wherever they were living the accommodation was provided by her employer.

You'd be forgiven for wondering why it matters, exactly which cottage and which set of fields they thought of as home. But I have a feeling it matters a great deal. There is a gap in Molly's history between about 1915 (when she left the Goggins) and 1920, when she married, and it's a gap that maps rather precisely onto the convulsive years between the First World War and the Irish War of Independence. My grandparents married in the middle of a war that – at least in some areas of West Cork – set Protestants loyal to the Crown at odds with Catholic neighbours. My grandfather chose to become a Catholic in an area and at a time when the two communities were at their most divided. It is hard to imagine a more difficult or more incendiary decision.

Molly and Tom got to know each other sometime around the beginning of the First World War, or the 1916 Rising in Dublin, or during the 1918 conscription crisis, when the threat of compulsory military service caused a huge backlash in Ireland, including a general strike, and encouraged the separatist movement. They became lovers during the War of Independence. They weren't, either of them, particularly engaged when it came to national politics. My mother remembers that in the 1940s her father used to vote for Clann na Talmhan, a party dedicated to the interests of small farmers. But politics happened to them anyway.

Political upheavals, military manoeuvres, men on the run, ambushes, informers, house-burnings, reprisals – it was all happening pretty much on the doorstep. Early in 1920 police stationed in outlying areas (and so vulnerable to attack by the IRA) abandoned their barracks and withdrew to the towns. Éamon de Valera, now leader of the Irish Republican government, had declared open season on members of the police force, describing them as 'spies in our midst'. The barracks at Ballydehob were evacuated and later destroyed. At the beginning of 1920 the courthouse was demolished by men wielding pickaxes; telephone wires were cut; the postal service attacked. By the summer of 1920, British government in Ireland was in a state of collapse.

The Crown responded to the collapse of the police force by building up a new paramilitary force, the Auxiliaries, made up of former officers in the British Army, and 'Black and Tans' – former soldiers from the lower ranks. The Restoration of Order Act, passed in the summer of 1920, gave these men almost limitless powers of arrest and court martial and opened the way for 'reprisals', or what one British politician called 'counter-murder': the deliberate killing of Republican prisoners and suspects, targeted raids, house-burnings, and the brutalization of the civilian population. County Cork was a hotspot for extrajudicial killings, raids and counterraids, especially after the county council pledged allegiance to the Republican Dáil Éireann in June 1920. The Auxiliaries placed towns in North and West Cork under curfew, and banned fairs and markets, further alienating the local population. In August Terence MacSwiney, the Sinn Féin elected representative for the Westminster constituency of Mid-Cork, who was also Lord Mayor of the city, was arrested and less than three months later he died on hunger strike. At the end of the year Auxiliaries set shops and buildings in the centre of Cork City alight and prevented the fire brigade from putting out the fires.

The trouble with all this 'background' is that it takes the place of the foreground. I see my grandparents disappearing under the weight of an established set of stories about West Cork during the War of Independence. Nearly everyone over a certain age with links to Ireland knows something about the

Kilmichael ambush, the burning of Cork, the assassination of Michael Collins on the road at Béal na Bláth. There would be a way of telling my grandmother's story by placing her directly in the centre of this revolutionary history, in relation to the men she knew, some of whom were actually famous, like her distant cousin Michael Collins. Or there's her brother Timmy, who died in France. A sort of rural Irish *Testament of Youth*. But it would not get me any closer to her.

It is not as though her own sense of her past was closely tied up with the Anglo-Irish War, or the Civil War, or even the First World War. Soldiering, political struggle, ideological battles over the Treaty – she never mentioned them. No one in her immediate family was a member of any political organization. When it came to 'history' her stories were about the Famine her parents had lived through as children, the behaviour of local landlords, neighbours who had gone to America, or who had come back again. It was all intensely local and familial.

The distinction I'm drawing here, between a female, domestic and familial set of concerns, and the story of revolutionary political action (men carrying arms, raids and counterraids, ambushes, spies, informers), only gets us so far, however. The 'big events' of the War of Independence and the Civil War in West Cork are surely a red herring. They are already so encased in story and counter-story they've become emblematic of war and revolution, rather than a window onto the unfolding experience of people's lives in 1919 and 1920. It's the small-scale stories, alive in the archive, told in statements to the Bureau of Military History, or in military pension files, that bring me closer to the ordinary experience of violence: the half-told stories of youthful enthusiasm for the Republican cause, neighbourly intimidation, bullying tactics, and the mistakes of which no one could be proud.

The local IRA battalion commander, Seán O'Driscoll, was

eight years younger than Molly, and more than twenty years younger than Tom. He was still in school in Ballydehob during the 1916 Rising, when he tried to blow up the local railway bridge with a single stick of gelignite. In September 1917, when he'd just turned eighteen, he set up a local branch of Sinn Féin with himself as Chairman, his friend from school as Vice-Chairman, and his sister as Secretary and Treasurer. It must have been hard to take him and his friends seriously. But by the middle of 1918 he was on the run and engaged full time (according to his own account) in organizing and training IRA volunteers into several battalions in the area. It was mostly small-scale stuff: raiding the local barytes mine for explosives; attacking the barracks at Ballydehob; raiding Protestant land-owners for arms. As more IRA men went on the run, the organization levied a fee (on a sliding scale) from local farmers, to pay for their support. 'The majority of the landowners in my company area (Ballydehob) were Protestants and pro-British,' O'Driscoll later explained, 'but all paid up their quota. In a few cases threats to seize stock to the value of the levy assessed were necessary before payment was made.'

Still, in 1920 a Protestant family, the Dalys of Lisheena-crehig, the townland where Tom had been living and working, was burnt out on suspicion of informing against the IRA. It is quite possible that Tom was working for the Dalys at the time. And on the morning my uncle Jackie was born, in Lissaclarig, where my newly married grandparents were living, a twenty-four-year-old Protestant, Samuel Shannon, was shot by the IRA for resisting an arms raid.

O'Driscoll doesn't claim responsibility for this murder in his account of gathering arms in the area. But the Cork Fatality Register, which lists all the deaths in the county due to the Irish revolution between 1919 and 1923, describes the event like this:

Shannon and his father Philip (aged about 62), a Protestant farmer at Lissaclarig, about 6 miles from Skibbereen, resisted an arms raid on the night of 10–11 September 1920 by ten to twenty armed and masked IRA men who tried to gain entry to their dwelling house. The raiders broke the door but were apparently driven off by the Shannons with sticks. Assuming that the intruders had left, the Shannons went out into their farmyard at about 7 a.m. on 11 September only to discover that the raiders had not departed. Samuel Shannon was shot at close range with a shotgun, with the full discharge entering his abdomen and causing terrible injuries from which he died a few weeks later at the South Infirmary in Cork city – on Friday, 1 October, at about 5 a.m. By that time his father had already sold the family farm at Lissaclarig.

The Shannons were close neighbours, and possibly also employers of Tom and Molly. Their farm was a substantial establishment, with stables, a coach-house, cow-houses, a dairy, two piggeries. They would have needed help beyond the labour provided by a daughter and two sons. Samuel Shannon was the youngest, four years younger than my grandmother. He and his family were members of the small congregation at the church Tom and his brother Stephen had attended for years, but that only Stephen attended now, because Tom had changed his religion a few months earlier.

Seven o'clock in the morning on 11 September 1920. It was a Saturday, and I can even find out from an historical weather chart that it had been a warm night. And perhaps for that reason the group of local Republicans – ten or twenty of them, probably mostly local but maybe some from further afield – had waited it out after their abortive raid on the Shannons' house the night before. At some point after the disturbance on the Friday night had died down (it was happening maybe half a mile away, or even closer), Molly must have gone into labour. She'll have sent Tom for her mother, or the local handywoman, when it got light. And then she'll have heard the gunshots and the screams, and wondered what was happening, and whether Tom was safe. He must have been suspect – all his life he had worked for Protestant farmers. He was certainly not a friend of the young IRA firebrands. But did they think he was an enemy?

In trying to get my head round what these events might have felt like I have a confused impression of shock and apprehension. The doctor called from town for Samuel Shannon, the labour pains, the women trying to get to Molly in time, the blood on the stones in the Shannons' yard, the sticks, the cart carrying Shannon's body to the road, the neighbours saying nothing about who was there or what they'd seen or what anyone had done. Men scattering; shotguns hidden in barns. The fear of who would be next, and the fear of reprisals. There is nothing heroic about these tales of revolution. They are for the most part grubby and disheartening stories of a war waged not against British forces, but against neighbours. The Shannons weren't the only Protestant family to leave in a hurry. All across the county between 1919 and the end of the Civil War in 1923 Protestant farmers, small and large, were selling up, almost all to their Catholic neighbours. And it was just at this point that my grandfather changed his allegiance. 'How did you believe it, Tom?' may also have meant, 'How could you have done it?'

14.

In the end Molly put on a blue suit to cover up her bulging belly and my grandparents were married. But she knew she was lucky. Sometime in the early 1940s a young neighbour drowned herself in the sea. When my mother, then in her early teens, asked her mother why she did it, my grandmother pursed her lips and said, 'She went out walking with a blackguard.'

My grandmother was lucky: that's one way of looking at it. She got the man she wanted in the end; she didn't have to leave to 'hide her shame', and she didn't have to put up with one-pair-of-boots. But maybe she wasn't lucky enough. She was forced to wait too long, so that everyone must have known about her 'lapse', however they interpreted it. And everyone would always know, including Arthur Murphy. That there was silence down the years doesn't mean that the pregnancy was secret – rather, I think, the opposite. Despite the fact that nothing was said openly, my grandmother would have to struggle for respectability.

Irish fiction and folklore are full of evidence of the lifelong stigma of illegitimacy, and its ability to 'stain' later generations. As one archive testimony puts it, 'When there'd be an out-fall or when they would start barging over the youngsters then you'd hear the pedigrees. "I wasn't born between a ditch and a holly bush . . . I wasn't born between a back door and a window shut".' This was what my grandmother was up against – and what she must have known Jackie would be up against. One historian of illegitimacy in Ireland notes that farmers 'would move heaven and earth to prevent their daughters marrying a bastard', unless he was well off. And it was even harder for women who were illegitimate to marry. A girl who was a 'bye-child' would, it was said, 'inherit the softness', the moral laxity, of her mother. One study estimates that in 84 per cent of cases of infanticide in the late nineteenth century the infants were illegitimate, but recently married couples also killed babies conceived before the wedding. The real stigma was sex, and it couldn't simply be undone by marriage.

Rather than thinking of my grandmother as someone marked out by her sexual probity – so much so that her sexuality was unthinkable to me – it must be more accurate to think of her as someone marked by sexual shame, at least in the early years of her marriage. Even if she had managed to keep the pregnancy secret until she was married, Jackie's birth three months after the wedding would have given the game away. It must have taken a superhuman effort of will to face down the talk.

Most couples in their situation married very quickly. And even when they managed to walk down the aisle within a couple of months of conception, they often left the area after the wedding, sometimes for years, until the gossip died down. But my grandparents stayed. My grandmother – sexually suspect, married to a Protestant – fought on the only front she knew: for respectability. Her family was going to be reputable, whatever the cost. They never missed Mass, or Holy Days, or failed in their myriad religious duties. They didn't borrow, they didn't owe, and they always paid their bill at the creamery. The house and garden were well kept, and apart from my grandfather's drinking, which, in reality, wasn't all that unusual, there was nothing for which they could be reproached. And slowly, over the years, the lapse was almost forgotten.

When, in 1931, they inherited the money from my great-uncle Jack's trucking concern in Massachusetts it must have felt like the struggles of the past really were in the past. They bought a farm, and stock. When my mother was two years old, the family of now five children moved a few miles from the rented labourer's cottage with its half-acre of garden (and the stream where Mary had drowned) to a 30-acre farm, and the solid two-storey stone farmhouse that went with it, a few miles away. Two horses in the stable, cows in the byre, a sow, chickens and their eggs, turkey-raising, taking milk to the creamery, growing wheat, growing potatoes. They became farmers, good neighbours, well-thought-of. Decent people, but not stuck up, who sheltered the 'school boys' and the men from the county home, and who could be relied on by Travellers for hot water, or the loan of an iron.

My uncle Jackie was twelve years old when his entire outlook changed. Until then, he had been able to look forward to a working life as a labourer much like his father – indeed he was probably already employed by the local farmers for odd jobs and for the harvest. But thanks to the money bequeathed from America the family were now property owners, and Jackie began to help his father run the farm that would one day be his.

But it was the fact that there was a farm to inherit at all that meant Jackie left Ireland for good. My Victorian grandparents had little to lose by marrying when Molly fell pregnant in 1920 – there was no land for anyone to worry over. But once there was a farm, there was a question of family inheritance and family respectability, and my grandmother was unable to see her way through to the other side of all that. There was having a name, and living up to it. As it turned out, clutching after respectability was the death of the farm anyway, because

Jackie was the one who loved the land, not his brothers. In the end the money from America was a curse not a blessing.

One answer to how my grandmother lived with her decision in the 1950s is that it wasn't really a decision at all. She was stymied by her own past. She could not bear to lose all she had fought for. She had worked so hard for her family's legitimacy. She knew – or she thought she knew – what it would be like to carry that shame and she could not face going through it all again. Was it worse that it was Jackie who was responsible for Lily's baby, rather than one of her other children? Jackie had been the embodiment of her own sexual shame. His birth had been what she had to live down. And now here he was again, proving he was just the same as his father. Proving she was just the same too.

One trouble with this interpretation of events is that it assumes a static historical backdrop – that illegitimacy was always shameful, and in the same way. But like pregnancy and childbirth the status of illegitimacy changes over time. Another way of thinking about this story is to take seriously my mother's description of her parents as Victorians. The pre-marital conception happened in 1920 but really it harked back to an earlier period – when getting pregnant before marriage was a route to marriage. Admittedly risky, but well tried. The kind of thing that couples whose union was approved of by the community might do, either because the match was already established, or because the woman wanted to secure it. This approach to marriage was probably still not all that unusual in the 1910s and 1920s, even if the Church thundered against sex much more strongly than in the sketchy pre-Famine, lackadaisical-Irish-Catholic past. My grandparents couldn't simply – or quickly – get married post-conception, since Tom had to be received into the Church, and that took time. But this requirement of 'turning' had only come into force during Tom's adulthood. It wasn't what he was used to, as a Victorian child, when all the grown-ups around him were married to people of the other faith.

If I interpret it this way then the pre-marital pregnancy and the long wait for the wedding were awkward rather than deeply shameful – and most probably it was a bit of both, depending on which neighbour you encountered on a trip to town or after Mass.

Thirty-five years later perhaps my grandmother felt justified in turning her back on Lily because this was not a union sanctioned by the two families and the wider community. She probably had no idea that Jackie and Lily were seeing each other, let alone anything more, until she was confronted with the evidence. No one was going to volunteer to be the bearer of that bad news. They were lovers, not a couple preparing for marriage, and that alone was enough to condemn them in her eyes. It is highly likely she saw absolutely no comparison between Lily's pregnancy and her own conception of Jackie. And she would have worked hard to keep the clear blue water between them. She needed to think of Lily as a schemer – an unsanctioned or illegitimate partner – out to marry her son and move her out of the way on the farm, because otherwise the similarities between them would be all too clear.

One thing this means is that her pre-marital conception of Jackie actually became more shameful over time, not less. It became more and more important, as her children grew to adulthood, that none of them knew she and their father had not kept to the same standards of chastity she expected of them. How would she have been able to explain herself if challenged? 'It was an accident'; 'things were different then'; 'we were planning to marry'? Or maybe even something closer to the truth: 'there was no farm to inherit'. She wouldn't have been able to claim she didn't know the sex was sinful. And none of it would have masked the hypocrisy of standing up for sexual probity now but not then. My mother, and perhaps too my mother's siblings, didn't challenge her. They knew she had no answer.

I have been assuming that living through the pregnancy in 1920 was hell, but that the shame and stigma slowly faded. It was hell but it was bearable, and for years she could put it behind her. What was not bearable at all was the possibility that her own children might learn of her lapse, as she must, at least sometimes, have suspected they had.

Stories 2

15.

I've spent months trying to figure out the story of my grandmother's pregnancies, typing names into search engines,
cross-checking birth dates, marriage dates, dates of death,
writing it all down. Can I really have spent all this effort on the
date of my grandparents' wedding? I'm bothered by a kind of
imbalance, between the weight of a story that wants to be
told, that keeps pulling me back to it – and its insignificance.
All this 'evidence', and what does it prove beyond the fact that
my grandparents weren't as well behaved as they were supposed to be. 'So what?' I keep thinking about these details of
my grandmother's life. What do they add up to? Why can't
I leave them alone? When my mother calls to pass on another
scattering of gingerbread crumbs I feel trapped. It's as though
I've been employed as a ghostwriter. But it's worse than that:
I'm compelled to tell a story on behalf of ghosts, that even the
ghosts don't understand. I am scrabbling around in the dark
with the dead and the missing, trying to make room for the
dead bodies that got buried, and the ones that got buried alive.

Take Maggie and Hannah in their corrugated-iron shop, and
their tale of the shadowy baby: the tale recently relayed to me
by my mother after a silence of nearly eighty years, concerning
my grandmother's supposedly lost child. None of it makes
much sense to me, yet I'm compelled to take account of it. It's
been handed to me as 'evidence', though of what I'm not sure,
and I can't simply discard it.

I've looked up Maggie and Hannah, of course. They were

born in 1883 and 1884, respectively. Their parents, who were born in the 1840s, were Irish speakers, who never learnt to read and write and who raised them in the poorest of the five houses in the townland of Glannakilleenagh. But the girls were moving beyond the cultural world of their parents. By her late twenties Hannah was running the shop that was owned by their neighbour Bridget Goggin – duties that demanded the skills of literacy and numeracy learnt in the local National School. This much can be deduced from the census form filled out in 1911 by Constable Denis O'Sullivan.

Bridget Goggin – the sense of something suddenly falling into place. The Goggins' farm was where Molly had lived and worked as a servant for some years before the First World War. So, the account of bartering butter and wartime information-gathering from Maggie and Hannah was not (or not only) a bizarre tale made up by my mother but a plausible story. It must have been when Molly was living with the Goggins that Maggie and Hannah got to know her. They were – all three – dependent on the Goggins financially, and Molly was also dependent on them for somewhere to live. Molly was the youngest of the three women by eight years, and the sisters took a shine to her – enough to be relied on thirty years later for sugar and tea off the ration. But what happened to give rise to this rumour of another baby, born before my grandmother married? My mother's ability to handle the vagueness is beyond me, although I have to consider the possibility that what she learnt from the sisters was simply too disturbing to hold on to in any detail. By contrast I want to know exactly what happened, and when.

I can puzzle out different scenarios. The first, and most obvious, is that Molly fell pregnant while she was at the Goggins'. Perhaps it was after her mistress Bridget died and she continued living with her two sons, for a time. Perhaps there was violence. Perhaps there was loneliness. Maggie and Hannah had watched the crisis unfold and were sorry for it.

But another possibility is that Molly fell pregnant while she was still living at home, and gave up the baby before she came to the Goggins, who took her in and gave her work after her family threw her out. This would account for the fact that Molly was living-in as a servant at all. Her family were farmers, not labourers, and it would have been far more usual for her to stay helping at home, even on a small farm. If this second scenario is true it would mean that by the time she was nineteen, when she is recorded in the census as living with the Goggins, my grandmother had already given birth to a baby, and lost it.

My grandmother's maiden name is common in the area but even so, when I searched the registry for illegitimate births (one clue is when the child's surname is recorded as the same as the mother's birth name) I came up with only three or four possible candidates in the whole country, over a period of fifteen years, and none of them seemed likely to have been my grandmother's lost baby.

And even as I dug around in the records I knew I was making a category error. All these stories and bits of evidence, which I was treating as clues to a history of unmarried motherhood in my family, were really traces of something much larger and more troubling: what it is to deny. All these silences, all these secrets, all these gaps – what they tell me is how the past was disavowed, how knowledge and understanding were buried so deep that all we have left are puzzles and enigmas.

What really went on in those conversations in Maggie and Hannah's shop in 1942 or 1943? They were women in their late fifties, talking to a girl of about thirteen. I imagine arcane circumlocutions. My mother, just a girl going out newly into the world by herself, trying to puzzle out the meaning, feeling knocked back by information she couldn't make sense of. Her mother, as a teenager, having sex. And even more disturbing, her mother, as a teenager, giving up a baby. Another sibling out in the world somewhere, out there all this time.

Like a late Freudian primal scene, did my mother just get it all wrong? Did she twist and turn to try to make sense of a series of heard and overheard clues? I've searched and searched, and gone down all sorts of online rabbit holes, but this baby is going to remain an enigma. Perhaps there was another baby, born more than a hundred years ago in a field somewhere in Ireland, or a house, and one way or another the baby was lost: dead or given away. Or perhaps the before-baby was just a rumour, a confused and misunderstood tale – a chimera patched together from the gossip that swirled about my grandmother when she fell pregnant with Jackie before she was married, and that the sisters, living far away from the ordinary day-to-day life of Molly's family as it unfolded over more than twenty years, had kept alive. This is surely the most likely explanation.

But one part of my grandmother's story keeps nagging at me: the old farmer with the hobnailed boots. In 1920 my grandfather was around to marry Molly, even though she had to wait for his conversion. It wasn't absolutely vital to find another match. But if Molly had first been pregnant some years earlier, with no prospect of anyone to marry her (not even a Protestant), her mother's despair at her rejection of the match makes an excruciating kind of sense. 'You'll never marry now!' meant: What are you going to do now, Molly? Your brother won't support you. Where are you going to go?

If my mother's Maggie and Hannah story is true, it allows me to recalibrate certain details of my grandmother's life.

It certainly looks like I've been reading things wrongly. All the moving about and living-in as a servant that I've been interpreting as the generalized effects of poverty make a different sense if that gap in Molly's history was filled with an unwanted pregnancy, being cast out from the family, a baby dead or given away.

My grandmother's favourite Arthur Murphy joke about the county home may also need to be recalibrated – perhaps she spoke as one who *had* been protected by the workhouse, long enough to make a new life. Perhaps her recommendation was not merely self-interested.

If my mother is right, my grandmother got pregnant twice outside of marriage, in a deeply conservative rural community where illegitimacy rates were – apparently – very low. Though I'm beginning to doubt the demographers who claim that Irish young people were unusual in their ability to refrain from sex. Everywhere you look: hidden babies. And I can't help thinking too that my young mother's nervous journeys up into the hills on her own had something to do with the story she imagined for her mother. The name Glannakilleenagh comes from the Irish Gleann na gCillíneach: glen, or valley, of the little burial grounds. She'll have known that, somewhere in the back of her head.

Because in the end the story tells me more about my mother than my grandmother. I am sure of this. It tells me about my mother's desire for a secret to keep. All around her, things left unsaid, knowledge she wasn't let in on. All around her, women sharing and keeping secrets. She wanted a piece of that. She knew there was a secret – or perhaps several secrets – her mother was keeping. She knew there were gaps in the story. Every night when the family prayed for Mary-that-died the silent complicity between her mother and her grandmother was re-enacted in front of the fire. And in all the years after her grandmother died, whenever Mary was mentioned, Molly bound herself to the secret again. Not to mention that whenever my mother's parents' marriage came up in conversation, something wasn't being said, and she knew it.

But she didn't know what the secrets were, so she made one to fit. That's why the Maggie and Hannah story is so lacking in detail – absent of narrative, absent of character. The story isn't accidentally a teenage story – a story belonging to a body becoming mature, intuiting the facts about sex and pregnancy. It's a teenage story because what girls learn on the cusp of womanhood is that there are things you don't talk about, especially with men around. Having secrets, and keeping them, is what grown-ups do. Secrets – and their corollary, gossip – make a woman of you. It's as though a woman's body can't grow up until it enters the world of secrets and secret-keeping.

Keeping sexual secrets was a necessary reaction to the premium placed on chastity in Ireland in the century after the Famine. It was a way of hiding from scrutiny. But it also offered a form of autonomy in a world where active choosing wasn't on offer for most women. Being in on a secret entails responsibility – for keeping it, or telling it. My mother believed that secrets were so empowering that she made one up. I know something you don't know I know. A negative power, certainly, but the best available.

And one thing is certain. True or not, the baby-before was knowledge my mother had in the 1950s, when she was called back home from her nursing training in England to attend to her mother's collapse on learning that Jackie had got a young neighbour pregnant. She came home to nurse a woman sick with shock, whom she knew had herself been pregnant before she got married, and whom she believed she knew had given up another baby before that. And she said nothing. It was a way of siding with her mother, without her mother knowing.

She's been siding with her ever since. My mother's stories are not innocent. The lesson she would like me to learn from them is that women's lives were difficult, that they had little choice in what happened to them, and we should not be too quick to judge when they fall short of our standards of natural justice. It strikes me that our roles have been reversed. I've got the archive and the documentary evidence. I can look things up and verify them, but she's the one behaving like the historian. 'They were Victorians,' she says, and she means they lived in another world from the one we know, and by other rules. She's saying, you've got to look at the context, you've got to understand the worldview that formed that generation before you judge them.

Inside the tolerance that my mother shows for that Victorian or Edwardian generation lies pity. Pity for lives that were hard, and pity that they knew no better. Both tolerance and pity imply a form of critique; a superior vantage point. We know better now, but we should not be too quick to judge people who didn't have our advantages.

But explaining why people behaved as they did is not the same as justifying their actions, or it shouldn't be. I can pity my grandmother, but that is no defence. When Lily became pregnant in 1954 the father of her baby was the boy my grandmother had conceived before marriage in 1920. I keep stumbling against that block. All through the 1960s and early 1970s, when my parents, my sisters and I were travelling 'home' from Coulsdon to the farm near Skibbereen, Mary was being subjected to the violence of the county home less than 25 miles away. How could my mother, my aunts and my uncles have acquiesced? How could Lily's parents, her aunts and uncles and siblings, have acquiesced? What good is pity without mercy?

16.

There is a common-sense account that explains why my cousin and her mother were cast out of their family and community and sent to Bessborough and then the county home. It goes something like this: thirty years after independence the role of religious institutions in managing social problems such as unmarried motherhood was accepted as normal (even if people like Arthur Murphy – people with experience of the institutions – still expressed their scepticism). The mother-and-baby homes had been operating 'successfully' for years and they were the natural or obvious answer to an unwanted pregnancy, even for those who had money and who entered as private patients. Put bluntly, in 1954 Bessborough offered a solution that simply wasn't available in 1910, still less in 1920, when even the workhouses weren't functioning. The system was cheap, and completely normalized. It would have been strange not to take advantage of it. Everyone else did.

I'd like to be able to work out the percentage of Irish families that were involved in some way with the institutions. It would be a big number. Thousands of Irish people had a daughter or a sister or an aunt who entered one of the homes, or who fled to England to avoid having to enter; or they had a son or a brother or an uncle who was responsible for a pregnancy; or they adopted a child from one of the homes; or they were that child who was adopted. But way beyond the number of people who were directly affected as victims and beneficiaries, the institutions reached into every corner of Irish life.

Think of all the daughters and sisters and aunts who worked in the homes as part of the convent hierarchy, the local priests who gained entry for their hapless parishioners, the bishops who oversaw the running of the homes, the priests who said Mass and heard Confessions.

The network of homes, orphanages, adoption agencies, reformatory and industrial schools was upheld by a vast state bureaucracy. The Commission of Investigation uncovered gruesome official paper trails involving literally hundreds of county council functionaries moving women from one institution to the next, arranging for the fostering out of babies, or bickering over the cost of the upkeep of the women and their children. The nuns provided their services for free, but there were still maintenance costs involved and nobody wanted to accept financial liability. The homes were funded by local councils and overseen by their health boards (which carried out regular inspections) and by local government departments. A baby might have been conceived in Mayo, but wasn't the mother from Sligo? Which council was responsible? There were social workers, child welfare officers, architects, building companies, contractors who worked out the cost of repairs to the sewers. Everything was reported on, minuted, filed. The mother of a friend of mine, now in her eighties, who worked for the local county council before she was married, found herself – more than once – filing the admission papers of girls she'd seen at dances a few weeks before.

When my uncle, my grandmother, and Lily's relatives handed Lily and her child over to the institutions they were doing what most people did. Admissions to the homes reached a peak in the 1960s, just at the point when in most countries refuges for unmarried mothers were closing down through lack of use. The Commission of Investigation cites this as evidence that the stigma of illegitimacy was slow to fade in Irish society, but it is just as clearly evidence of the continuing failure of the state to help lone mothers. Contraception was illegal in the south of Ireland between 1935 and 1979 and afterwards hard to access. Until 1973 there was no unmarried mother's allowance – no financial help whatsoever for a single mother and her child. When abortion became legal in Britain in 1967, the harsh regime in the Irish mother-and-baby homes began to relax, and six-month, rather than two-year stays, became the norm. But the main reason for this was to stop women and girls going to England and accessing abortions, rather than any concern for their welfare.

The shift in circumstances from my grandmother's extramarital pregnancy in pre-independence Ireland, to that son's fathering of a child in the mid-1950s, was the result of a series of long, slow, historical changes. The decline of an Irish-speaking peasantry after the Famine, and the development of an English-speaking culture of small peasant-proprietors determined to hold on to their land; the slow disappearance of folkloric traditions and a relaxed attitude to organized religion in favour of extreme displays of devotional piety and adherence to Catholic doctrine ('the best Catholics in the world!'); distrust of official institutions run by British overseers (the law, the judiciary, the workhouse system) replaced by growing confidence in religious-run social services: the mother-and-baby homes and the industrial schools; tolerance of mixed marriages and even 'invalid' marriages giving way to moral condemnation.

Life for the rural poor was lived mostly under the official radar in Victorian and Edwardian Ireland. People's behaviour might be highly regulated, but according to familial and community norms, not state norms. The people with local influence on families were the matchmakers, not the social workers. I think of my grandfather repeatedly hauled up before the petty sessions, or local magistrates' courts, for minor misdemeanours: less a sign that he was particularly feckless than that people routinely ignored the authorities. When my grandmother got pregnant in 1920 she was living in a highly regulated society, but there was no state-sanctioned bureaucracy ready to 'manage' the social problem she represented.

By the 1950s communities had become inured to exceedingly high levels of official surveillance, at the hands of schoolteachers, priests, nuns, guards and an army of local government functionaries. By the middle of the twentieth century the population of the Irish Republic was probably the most institutionalized in the world. It had not only the highest admission rate to mother-and-baby homes in Europe, but by far the largest percentage of the population in psychiatric hospitals. Then there are the numbers institutionalized in the Church. In the mid-1960s one in ten Irish children entered a religious life, as priests, monks, or nuns (committing, supposedly willingly, to the chastity which those sent to mother-and-baby homes were perceived to have disregarded). Some seminaries took children from their parents at the age of eleven. Add to this reformatories, industrial schools, boarding schools, boarding out: to a unique extent Irish children were not at home with their parents, and this is before we account for the impact of emigration. Like the women sent to mother-and-baby homes, most Irish emigrants were young adults, but a child doesn't stop being somebody's child when they reach adulthood. Arguably, the rhetoric of the Irish family was a smokescreen for the relative absence of the family as a private sphere of emotional and affective ties.

Bessborough provided several services – not only did the

home offer a hiding place for Lily's pregnant body, and later for her baby, but it allowed my grandmother, and Jackie, to shift responsibility away from their own lack of care to the institution.

The institutional regime at Bessborough was built on an already well-established structure of disavowal. Families were already highly practised at not seeing what they could see, and not knowing what they knew. This habit of silence was one thing that did not change over the years. But that habit became dangerous when it got institutional backing. Turning a blind eye to sexual indiscretion in 1920 was, or could be, enabling. It meant you could get on with finding a private solution. But the mother-and-baby homes, and the intricate state-sanctioned local government machinery that kept them going, took secrecy out of the hands of individuals and bureaucratized it. In the 1950s there was a panoply of public institutions that seemed explicitly designed to help families negotiate their most intimate problems. It was a Faustian pact. In shielding people like my grandmother and Lily's parents from talk, they also shielded them from care.

Missing Persons

17.

I've delivered a damning verdict on the behaviour of almost everyone involved in the crisis that unfolded in the autumn of 1954, apart from Lily. But I'm conscious that I am judging with the benefit of hindsight. I know how badly it all turned out. If I am going to be fair to my uncle, and to Mary's grandparents on both sides, I need to acknowledge that they couldn't have predicted what was going to happen – or not the whole of it. Everyone must have been banking on adoption – newly legalized only the year before – as the solution to this inconvenient baby. Perhaps they all thought it would be over in a year or two. The baby would go to America, Lily would return home or make a new life in England, and when it was all over Jackie would be able to come back and take over running the farm again. But it didn't work out that way. There was no adoption and no moment when it was all over.

Did my uncle Jackie understand that the decision he was making to leave Lily meant he must leave everything else too – his own family, the farm that had recently been transferred into his name following the death of his father, his whole way of life – and for good? Would he have done things differently if he had known what would happen?

There is a certain irony in the fact that the most missing person of all in this story is Jackie. Because Lily and Mary were sent to institutions there are documents to be consulted – a paper trail, however scanty. Years ago, when I visited the Convent of Mercy in Clonakilty, I was able to look at the record of admission for my cousin, and in the end talk to a nun who had known her. Meanwhile Jackie has all but vanished. In this too my family story is just like everyone else's. The men who were responsible for getting their girlfriends pregnant were often able to disappear (though not all of them did, of course). There was a whole system set up that made disappearing look ordinary.

It was just so easy to leave – a £5 ticket for the boat, and the excuse of plenty of work in England. All across the country people were taking the boat to find paid labour, so there was no need for an explanation. The Irish newspapers were full of doom-laden stories of towns and villages emptying, and it was true that as more and more people left it became harder for those who stayed to make a living. Shopkeepers lacked customers, teachers lacked children to teach, farmers lacked labourers, sports teams lacked players, women lacked men to marry, men lacked women. By the early 1960s one-sixth of the Irish-born population – and a vastly greater proportion of men and women of working age – were living and working in England. My mother was one of those emigrants, and we were living in England too. But Jackie still managed to go missing.

I don't know whether I ever met my uncle Jackie, or only heard about him in tiny snatches of talk. He was always off somewhere, at the edge of things. My memories of my uncles feel very like photographs, or grainy stills taken from an old film long since lost: tiny slices of time frozen into a visual scene, but lacking speech, context and background narrative. It would be impossible to reconstruct the plot of the film from these images. There is a pub somewhere in Shepherd's Bush (but it could as easily be Kentish Town, or Cricklewood), with bench seats covered in black vinyl. My uncles are there but I am not sure which of the men in dark suits (there seem to be a lot of

them) are related to me. I can conjure Guinness and Jameson whiskey and cigarettes, the taste of Tayto crisps and red lemonade, and the sound of voices. But they are not really part of the memory. The memory is black vinyl (a corner bench, I think) and dark suits. It is the sense of men – not family men, like fathers and grandfathers, but men as men. A sense made up of the smell of Sunday suits, stubble, men's soap and the various unfamiliar odours of the public bar, but also the size of them, gathered together, drinking and talking and making noise.

This memory has lodged itself in my consciousness because the experience was unusual. When I was small, children weren't allowed in pubs in England. When my parents went for a drink on a Sunday, after Mass, at the social club attached to the hospital where my mother worked, we got to go in too, and play billiards or put records on the jukebox. This was because it was a club, with paid membership, and not a pub. But mostly, if they wanted a drink, we had to stay in the car. We got bottled drinks and crisps brought out to us, and we annoyed one another by jostling for space on the vinyl seats of the Vauxhall Viva estate, instead of annoying other people. Often we had the dog with us, ears cocked and with his nose to the open gap in the window, as we used him as a cushion, or burrowed into his fur. But the Irish landlord of the pub where my uncle Thomas drank ran his establishment as a sort of legal outpost of home – a place where children were allowed. Still, my guess is he didn't get many kids turning up. The public bar was for men. They drank there after work, and on Sundays, and for many of them the pub was a refuge from their spartan lodgings and shared rooms. There must have been women too, at the edges of this social scene, but it mainly offered a space for single men. I've remembered it because at some level I knew I wasn't supposed to be there.

Uncles weren't fathers – that much was obvious. For a start they didn't have children with them. That they might have children and not live with them, or even not know them, was a possibility I hadn't yet encountered. They were also far more indulgent with sweets and treats than any father I knew. The fathers of my schoolfriends and neighbours were distant in a different way from the uncles. They wanted a break from us. But the uncles could afford to be easy-going. They were unencumbered. In addition to no children, as far as I could tell, the uncles didn't seem to have their own homes, or partners, or cars – or if they did, we never saw them. Uncles projected an active sense of not-being-fathers, and of not having a family role. As proof I can point to a photograph of my parents' wedding, taken in Coulsdon in September 1955. The group stands a bit awkwardly about, in a line – my father's relatives on one side, somewhere towards the middle my grandmother and, after a sizable gap, my uncles Jackie and Thomas. They look wildly out of place in this English scene of suburban family bonding. Jackie in particular. He stands like the farmer he was, legs wide, arms behind his back. He's too large, and his clothes are all wrong. His stance says, I do not belong.

It is only now that I sit down to think about this photograph that I realize it was taken a few months after the crisis back home over Lily's pregnancy. That is why my uncles are in the picture at all. They had left Ireland for London sometime in the spring of that year, around the time that Lily went into Bessborough Mother and Baby Home in Cork.

Something is missing from the story of that Christmas in 1954. It was November when my mother got home. She found my grandmother prostrate with distress. It is obvious too that she was furiously angry, and it appears that she displaced at least part of her anger with her son onto Lily – she made clear that she did not want Lily moving onto the farm to live in her house. My mother suggests that Lily's father didn't make it any easier by (apparently) claiming he'd have Jackie's farm: 'I'll take every field and hen from him.' He seems to have been more interested in the farm than in his daughter, because he didn't offer her or her baby support. The only option for Jackie and Lily was to leave, either together or apart. The decision not to marry must have already been made before my mother got home – that was why there was scandal, after all, rather than a shotgun wedding. But what is missing is the reason why.

Perhaps it's simple – Jackie was unwilling to take on a wife and child, and he preferred a life on his own if he was going to have to leave the farm. Perhaps it's darker than that. Perhaps the sex wasn't consensual, and there was no way of repairing the relationship. When I try to disentangle what went on back in 1954, I can't help thinking in terms of 'choice' and decision. I wonder whether Jackie and Lily decided together that they would go their separate ways and that Lily would put the baby up for adoption (an adoption that never happened). Or whether it was Jackie's decision to take no responsibility for the child that left Lily without options. But I worry that in looking for reasons I am asking the wrong questions. It may not have felt like choice was part of the landscape at all.

Everyone was home that Christmas, including Jackie's brothers Stephen and Thomas, who had been working as build-ers' labourers in Dublin. By the end of the holidays it had been established – perhaps without clearly speaking of it – that Stephen would stay home to look after the farm, Jackie and Thomas would go to England, and Lily would go to Cork. Jackie never returned.

My mother was living at the time in the nurses' home at Whipps Cross hospital, and she found Jackie and Thomas a room with a landlady not far away in Leytonstone. This small fact – that she had found their first digs – is something I have known as long as I can remember, and I have known it as a story of her success. She met her brothers at Euston early on a Sunday morning and took them to the house where the land-lady had prepared a good roast dinner, and they were pleased. The nice bit of meat – it was an odd detail, especially when part of an ordinary tale of moving to London for work, but now I understand it to stand in for so much. Jackie had traded in his livelihood, the farm he had inherited, his bond with his mother and several of his siblings (whom he would never see again), his relationship with Lily and with his future child – for what? Freedom from responsibility? He was thirty-four years old, and he was going to have to start from scratch, as a labourer on building sites, and a seasonal agricultural hand. I imagine the journey over on the boat, and then the train. It must have been easier that Thomas was with him – on a journey to see what England was like. But under the jokes and the drink-fuelled bravado the sense of waste was surely palpable, and my mother must have felt it too. Jackie was ten years older than she was, and had long been a working farmer. For nearly ten years since their father had died Jackie had been the head of the family. She must have felt a sense of responsibility in find-ing him a new home. The hot dinner that Sunday became a sort of talisman for her – a sign that she had played her part in managing the transition from the old life to the new.

I heard about the hot dinner but not the reason why it meant so much. Most of my mother's stories about her brothers were like this – anecdotes and curtailed stories, like yellowing snap-shots with no connection to before or after. I learn from their form, not their content, that the relationships were severed. Over the years, as her brothers moved between lodgings in different towns, and no one was given to writing letters, they lost touch. My mother's stories are memories that can't be brought into conversation with the present.

Jackie died in the autumn of 1972, when he was fifty-two years old. He was living at the time in digs in Bury St Edmunds. He went out hunting with his dog and never returned. After some days his landlady contacted the police and discovered that he had been 'BID', brought in dead, to the hospital, after a massive heart attack. He had nothing on him to identify him. I imagine his pockets contained a roll of notes – his wages from farming and building work – and tobacco. Eventually the police turned up at our door in Coulsdon and my mother went to identify the body. She spoke to the mortuary assistant. He said that from the state of his heart he must have worked hard as a young man.

And that is about all I have to go on, in imagining my uncle's life in England. A picture of him taken in 1955, a death notice from 1972, and a remembered conversation with a mortuary assistant. The death notice comes in a long list which records the date and place of all the people who died that autumn in Suffolk, alongside their date of birth. In Jackie's case the date of birth is listed as 'about 1920' and it almost makes me smile. Jackie had been living under the radar – he didn't need a passport, since he never went home, and (I'm guessing) he didn't register with any national or county authority, to avoid paying tax on his earnings. He'd never handed his birth certificate in to anyone. He had probably never seen it himself.

The habit of working on building sites and engineering projects under assumed names was common practice – expected, even. If you worked for less than two years in England you could claim tax exemption, but that meant that if you intended to stay longer you had to keep changing your identity. You could get caught out if you weren't up to speed about who you were supposed to be and how long you'd been in England as that person. During the 1970s the Inland Revenue people took to stopping lorryloads of workmen on the roads and taking down names. As another of my uncles, Jimmy, remembered, you'd need your wits about you. He kept a small notebook in which he recorded and then memorized the various periods he was supposed to have been back in Ireland, and the names and dates of the people he'd been in England. When he was checked in the back of a lorry on the road he was in the clear.

There are plenty of stories like this, of labouring men in the 1960s and 1970s getting one over on the tax inspectors, by changing their names, or by making up wives and children back home (for a better tax code). 'How many children do you have? I mean for the tax . . .' These accounts are mostly couched in a mock-heroic mode – as though the matter of economic survival in Britain was a huge joke, a case of pitting the fearless and canny Irishman against the might of the looming indus-trial state machine. But the costs of anonymity were huge too – it meant no national insurance and an insecure pension, for a start, and no payout if you got injured or killed on site. The unnamed can disappear all too easily, and there's often an underlying elegiac note to these stories of men taking risks with their identities, for cash. In Timothy O'Grady's fictional-ized documentary account of a Donegal labourer in England, *I Could Read the Sky*, one character plumps for the name Joe on a job in Suffolk. Joe is also the name of his uncle, who has disappeared:

> In the beet factory in Ipswich I took the name J. Brady after the
> name was written in the back of the coat Ma bought me at the
> Fair. When the paymaster asked me what the J stood for I

nearly said Jupiter because I was thinking of P. J. and his desire for a telescope. But I said 'Joe' in time. Each Sunday morning after Mass I went to a different place for a drink but no one had heard of Joe. 'What other names did he use?' asked a man from Tipperary.

Living in England under a false name is one thing; but dying under a false name means you may never be found.

Jackie was what we would now call an undocumented migrant, but the term seems anachronistic. It seems truer to say he was living an itinerant life, taking work and pleasure where he found them. His brother Thomas was eight years younger. He was twenty-six when he arrived at the landlady's house in Leytonstone, and better fitted – or so it must have seemed at the time – for this nomadic life. Thomas had spent time working in Dublin, and he had learnt the skills of stone-cutting and bricklaying. An easy-going man, familiar with living with strangers, and working for a wage. He queued for work on street corners in Camden Town in the early morning; he went across the country working for large engineering companies like Costain and Laing: digging drains, laying cables, shovelling muck and pouring concrete. He sent money home to his mother – and sometimes to his younger sister, my mother, to help her buy clothes and extras for the four of us. I remember a little dark-blue, corduroy dress that I associate with him, though I know the choice of that dress in particular is arbitrary. It had a scalloped white collar and a tiny brooch, in the shape of a hedgehog, pinned to it.

By the early 1970s Thomas was living in a room in Kentish Town, and still regularly sending £5 back to his mother. He drank a good deal of his spare cash in the local pubs; he ate his dinner in cafes, and occasionally had a flutter on the dogs or horses. A lot of accounts of labourers' broken health focus on the rain: working without protection in all weathers, and no way of properly drying out. Sitting soggy in the pub all evening rather than feed the gas meter, pulling on wet clothes in the morning, you ended up living in a kind of endless damp. But it was the heat that got Thomas. One day in the burning summer of 1976 he was working on a site in London when he felt unwell. He found a quiet spot where he sat by himself to eat the sandwiches he had brought for lunch, but when they went to call him back to work he was dead. He was forty-seven years old.

18.

My uncles' lives would be even more of a blank except that the emigrant world they lived in was a source of fascination for the Irish at home, and they wrote about it. They even experimented with it. A spell working on building sites in England was almost a rite of passage for young Irish men from the 1960s through to the 1980s, whatever their background. The sons of shopkeepers and better-off farmers went for a stretch, to see what it was like and to save some money for a house, or machinery. Middle-class boys whose fathers were doctors and lawyers did a stint in their university holidays, while their sisters worked in hotels and restaurants. Nearly all the Irish writers who made their name in the 1960s had some experience of living or working with labouring men in England – John B. Keane, Tom Murphy, Richard Power, Brendan Behan and his brother Dominic, Anthony Cronin, John McGahern. And there was Dónall Mac Amhlaigh, who did things the other way round. He went to Northampton in 1952, to a job as a stoker in a hospital, because there was no work for him at home in Kilkenny. But he quickly moved on to a series of labouring jobs, including working in an iron foundry, digging tunnels, and laying underground cables at the American base at Brize Norton. And in the evenings he wrote about his experiences, in Irish, in a series of notebooks that he eventually published in the early 1960s as *Dialann Deorai*. It later appeared in translation as *An Irish Navvy: The Diary of an Exile*. He was a labourer first and a writer second.

The focus in nearly all these accounts is on the hardship endured by the long-stay labourers, and their resilience in the face of it: the harsh working conditions, the brutality of the (mostly Irish) foremen, the lack of home life, the camaraderie and friendships between men, the competitive feats of physical strength – a man lifting a sack of cement with his teeth; one man challenging another to see who could empty coal from a skip quickest, who could dig furthest, fastest. The stories tend to feature prodigious amounts of fighting (particularly in the 1950s), prodigious amounts of drink, and a surprising number of practical jokes. But underneath it all is a base note of sadness. They would be at home if they could.

I've researched and written about these narratives for years, but there's something that keeps nagging at me. It has to do with an uncomfortable mixture of tragedy and pride that gets injected into these stories. Men like John B. Keane (the son of a teacher) and Richard Power (a Trinity College graduate and translator) encountered a world in Birmingham and Northampton that was largely alien to them, and although they wrote about it sympathetically, it was still alien. They could see, even at the time, how these men had been sacrificed to an existence without a future, unless they were lucky enough to get out early. The prevailing mood in contemporary accounts is a kind of pathos. The labourers are figured as giants laid low, but at the same time as men determined to survive *as Irishmen* in England. The self-destructive behaviour, the binge culture, the bravado with which a man might drink his week's wages in a night – it all said, 'I am living for the present', not the future. They were not simply 'making the best of things', but determined to behave as though, freed of ties and responsibilities, they were actually having the best of things.

There was a boldness to men like my uncles' refusal to count the cost of their way of life – but the plays and stories encouraged the audience to do the counting for them. We know what consequences lie beyond the decision to neither go home, nor settle anywhere else, and as an atmosphere of tragic waste builds up around them, the itinerant labourers begin to stand for more than themselves. The hardships of their lives in England are a kind of metaphor for all Irish hardship; they are late versions of the nineteenth-century Irish emigrant, plangent figures of loss and disconnection.

The air of loss in which they seem to move has a lot to do with the fact that they don't speak much. When Philip Donnellan made a documentary about Irish manual labourers for the BBC in 1965, he couldn't find many men who would talk to him – so his film focuses on faces and bodies instead. A huge arm wields machinery digging the London Underground; a man almost disappears under the mound of clay he has dug out of the ground, his jacket flung to one side as he works. In this film the faces of the men, and their bodies, do the speaking, alongside a musical soundtrack made up of lyrical ballads of privation and yearning. The singing voice stands in for emotions that can't be spoken, and which mostly seem to come down to 'a feeling of terrible longing', as the critic John Berger said of these men.

Too much longing would feminize them however, and in the films and stories it's tempered by humour (the practical jokes), by anger, or resignation. It's the resignation that lends this way of life its heroic aura. In reality, numbers of Irish labourers in Britain did join unions, and went on strike for better pay and conditions. But the stereotype is of men who held themselves aloof from labour organizations just as much as from domestic life. Films like *The Irishmen* and, later, *I Could Read the Sky* conjure a certain reverence for their stoicism, although this is stoicism expressed as anything but, of course. Drinking and fighting and gambling aren't high on the list of recommendations for cultivating patience, fortitude and a calm acceptance of a destiny you can't change. England is both enemy – the industrial power that is leaching the life away from rural Ireland – and saviour, in that in England a way of life is possible, even if it's one that leads nowhere.

I watch these slow-moving films in a kind of emotional frenzy that seems wholly inappropriate to their tone. I can feel the powerful undertow of that tide of pathos, pulling me under. The silent faces say, this is our fate, and it seems almost disrespectful of me not to salute their proud resignation. But I fight back. Feelings of pity and reverence for my uncles don't bring them closer; they push them further away. I'm much more taken with a series of short documentary newsreels made for Irish television by a Catholic organization called Radharc ('Vision', or 'Scene'), funded by the archbishop of Dublin in the early 1960s. You can find some of their documentary shorts online: men arriving at Euston with little clue of what they are going to do or how they are going to live; women and men working in large hotels near Paddington; men living in a camp and building a nuclear-power station at Oldbury on the River Severn in 1965. The interviewers are mostly priests, wearing priestly kit, but the men talk back, in a mostly matter-of-fact way, about the work and why they are doing it. The questions are framed around the loss of family and community. 'Do you find it lonely?'; 'How do you look to the future?' Men number the children they have left at home, and their ages. 'The longing is for home,' says one. 'When will you go back?' asks the priest. 'Ah, we'll see later.' And the contradictions are glaring. One man who has six children at home, aged between five and eighteen, has seen them once a year for ten years. He says he'll

do another year or eighteen months in England, because he doesn't want to miss his children growing up. There's absolutely no chance, he says, that he would bring his family over to settle with him, because no one gives a thought for 'family unity' in England.

The voiceover to the Donnellan film describes the men as 'nomads', but it's a rare interviewee who admits that his plan is to stay roaming in England. One day they'll be back is the refrain. 'Many of them have grown old waiting for the day they would return, a day that never dawned for them. Some have remained unmarried, others have spent the best years of their lives separated from their wives and family.'

There was no television in the farmhouse where my grandmother lived with Stephen, after all the others had gone. But I think I know how she would have responded to this film if she had seen it on the television, in that autumn in 1965. She would have been scanning the faces, to see if her sons were there. I know, because I do it too. I try to match the photographs in my head to the images on screen, of men crowding out through a door, moving between the huts, or sitting in the canteen and turning to smile and nod into the camera. The man who has left his six children at home is (from his accent) from Cork, or from Kerry, and his long face looks familiar. It's a handsome, rangy face. He looks a bit like an actor playing the part of an itinerant labourer. I want to ask him, did you come across Jackie and Thomas? What did you think of them? I watch the scenes of work on the M1 and the London Underground in Donnellan's film (made around the same time, in 1965). I watch them again and again. I slow the film to half-speed. I scan it frame by frame. I am looking for my uncles to look back at me. I have the thought that perhaps I could simply choose one or two of them and make them mine.

Then again, I've a suspicion that all the attention given in films and books to these single men labouring in England was a form of displacement activity. Tom Murphy's brilliant play about a family of brothers in Birmingham, *A Whistle in the Dark*, was staged in London in 1961, when Murphy was twenty-six years old. He wrote it following a summer in Birmingham in 1958, spent living and working on building sites with his own brothers – he was the youngest of a family of ten. The play offers a harrowing account of the deformations that class wreaked upon the dispossessed in the West of Ireland, and their destructive rage against the system that has failed them – both in Ireland and in England. Murphy wrote the play at his kitchen table in Tuam, down the road from the concrete lids of the Mother and Baby Home's sewerage system. Nothing was being said, by Murphy or anyone else, about the women and children in the homes, and, apart from a few campaigning voices, very little was being said about the women who emigrated. The destruction that was being inflicted on families by the authorities that ran the homes, the people who oversaw them, and the communities that used them couldn't be acknowledged. The Radharc documentary weighs the scales in the other direction: the men are missing out on their families, but the wives and children are still there at home to come back to, if only there was the money.

Or I could turn to the haunted face of actor Jack MacGowran in Samuel Beckett's play for television, *Eh Joe*, first broadcast on the BBC in July 1966, when I was three years old and being photographed by my father in front of a porch in the West of Ireland. 'Thought of everything? . . . Forgotten nothing?' the female voice whispers into Joe's ear as the camera moves slowly closer to his bewildered, tortured features. Joe is trapped in his room with this commentary that he cannot stop. He tries his best to shut it out. Full of accusation, it's the voice of a woman who has been seduced and left by Joe. 'The best's to come, you said, that last time . . . Hurrying me into my coat . . . Last I was favoured with from you.' She tells the story of another woman's suicide, after Joe has abandoned her, recounting in exacting detail the young woman's failed attempts to kill herself (drowning doesn't work, the razor doesn't work . . .) and her eventual success. 'There's love for you,' she says. Here's a different story, one of men living in bare rooms in digs and trying to escape from their past, rather than longing to get back to it.

It's hard to tell who the voice belongs to. Is it Joe's inner conscience? Is it Beckett's? The room with its single bed looks like an austere version of any labourer's lodgings, but it's also an archetypical Beckettian stage – empty of everything except a man, alone and imprisoned with and by his own thoughts.

Beckett wrote the play during the early years of his long affair with Barbara Bray, which was painfully tolerated by his wife Suzanne (as his other affairs were tolerated by both Suzanne and Barbara). 'Eh, Sam?' he asks. Have you used these women? Have you destroyed them?

Jack MacGowran was around the same age as my uncle Jackie (and he died not long after him too), but apart from that I don't think they had much in common. I know that the actor Jack MacGowran in the film isn't actually someone called Joe, just as he isn't Sam, and he isn't Jackie either. I don't know if he brings me any closer to Jackie or not.

Were my uncles saying yes, or were they saying no to the family system? By disappearing into England they were re-linquishing any claim to the farm, and accepting that they wouldn't rear a family at home, if at all. Looked at in one way, they were leaving the way clear, despite the cost to themselves. Or here's another way of thinking about them – an alternative to the tragical–stoical story. They chose itinerant lives; they said no to marriage, family and farm. I could go

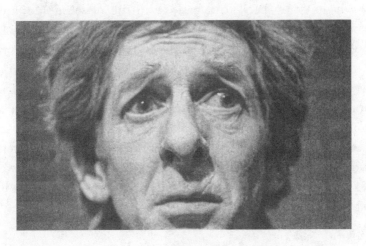

further. They pleased themselves! They were feckless and sloughed off responsibility. Perhaps, when choices are so limited, the only freedom you can exercise is to refuse to choose.

Jackie's departure for England – his refusal of responsibility – meant that the duty to look after the farm, and support my grandmother, passed to his brother Stephen. The farm was put in Stephen's name, but this doesn't mean he wanted it. He was landed with it, with no capital to invest in improving it, and – although I remember him as always the gentlest of men – he made his passive resistance felt. He farmed half-heartedly and drank whole-heartedly. He was, my mother says, probably gay. When I asked her why she thought so her response was faltering. Her evidence seemed mostly to be based on his kindness, and (she was embarrassed by the inadequacy of this as proof of anything) that he talked to girls. She stumbled about looking for a way to say he wasn't a boy like other boys in rural Ireland in the 1930s. It was one of those moments when the pain to which she had been witness, which she had felt powerless to do anything about, really was unspeakable. At any rate, whatever he suffered, he suffered in silence.

I keep going back to a passage in the novelist Édouard Louis's account of his father's murder at the hands of the French political system. It's a report on the social death of a man, and a class, caused by poverty, exhausting manual labour, poor health care, lack of education, lack of opportunity, lack of a youth and the humiliation of lacking all these things. There is something he wants to try to put into words, Louis says. It is the idea of a life lived in the negative. Jean-Paul Sartre asked whether we are defined by our inner being, or by the things we do and the actions we take. But, Louis wants to know, what if we are what we haven't done? What if the world, or society, has stood in the way so that doing is all but impossible?

My uncles Jackie and Thomas – but also Stephen, who stayed at home – lived their lives in the negative. Freedom, in the sense of opportunity, and choice, wasn't available to them – or to be more precise, their choices were extremely limited. That is one of the reasons my mother's stories about her brothers were so curtailed. It wasn't simply that there was hardly anything to tell about their daily lives once they were labouring in England, and what there was she didn't know to tell. It was also that if she spoke of them, she would have to speak of that absence – of the lack of the freedom and choice that is so central to our twenty-first-century conception of what it means to live a life (to have a life story to tell), that she knew we would not understand. I say 'we' but really I know that of her daughters it was only me that wouldn't leave this alone, who kept knocking on the door of this history and asking to be let in.

Jackie was never going to survive navvying in Camden, or pouring concrete on the large engineering jobs, the motorways, dams and power stations. After a few years he cut out and headed for agricultural labouring work – the kind of work he knew well – in Essex and Suffolk. There he caught the tail end of the slow decline of centuries of traditional farming customs and communities. The people were different; the soil was different; the crops and even the animals were somewhat different. But the seasons were much the same, and perhaps something about the rhythms of everyday life felt familiar, and safe.

I imagine he spent time pulling beet near Ipswich, but I hope he managed to keep out of the beet factories, where the crop was pulped for animal feed. I imagine that was soul-destroying work. I imagine he walked long distances between villages and offered his services to farmers he met along the way.

I imagine he was pretty good with horses, and he could drive a straight furrow, if he came across an old-timer who hadn't the money to hire a tractor for the ploughing. And I am pretty sure that he worked at road mending, drainage and ditch clearing for the county council in the winters.

I imagine he didn't miss the no electricity, no plumbing and no heating at home. The damp, the tin bath in front of the fire filled from the kettle, the turf smoke, the sputtering oil lamps. But I imagine he missed the card games, the fair days, the turkey drives, walking out in summer after Mass and maybe, even, the Stations held at the house, with all the flurry of preparation for visitors: clearing out, whitewashing, the girls baking.

I imagine he loved the ancient Suffolk woodlands – nothing like the bare hills and stone walls at home. I imagine he missed cutting turf on the bog, for the sociability of it. He missed the furze, and the fuchsia, the flag irises in June and montbretia in August. I imagine he didn't miss bog water up to his knees, the clay soil stuck to his boots, and the lashing rain coming in over the Atlantic. I don't know whether he thought of his fields, gone now to rushes.

I imagine he hated fish and chips. Actually, I know this, because my mother told me – the last time she saw him, some-time in the late 1950s, he was living in Southend-on-Sea and he complained about the awful food. They laughed about it.

He must, somehow, have got a licence for a shotgun, though I've found no record of it, nor, come to think of it, of a dog licence either. I imagine he was pretty good at staying under the radar. I imagine if he brought rabbits home his landlady didn't know how to skin and prepare them, so he'd have shown her. I imagine she liked him.

I imagine he had black moods when he cursed his situation. And I imagine he forgot about it after.

I imagine he wasn't alone. There were others like him – men washed in from elsewhere who were finding spaces for themselves in the vestiges of an agricultural system that depended on men more than machines. Further north, in Lincolnshire, seasonal labourers from Donegal had kept the agricultural economy going for more than a century, by moving through the county with the harvest. There were several lyrical accounts of traditional farming in Suffolk written during the 1950s and 1960s, and I turn to them for glimpses of the way of life Jackie would have found there. George Ewart Evans, a Welsh teacher who settled in Blaxhall, north of Ipswich, wrote a series of lovingly detailed portraits of the traditions and customs that were all but disappearing around him. Evans mixed oral histories taken down from elderly neighbours, studies in folklore and etymology, and research in local diaries, school records, estate accounts and other documents. He was interested in deep England. He traced the roots of farming practices back to the seventeenth century, in some cases, and there is no evidence of itinerant labourers, Irish or otherwise, in his Suffolk. Either he couldn't see them, or they weren't there, but I incline to the former.

It's the same with Ronald Blythe's luminous description of several generations of village life in East Suffolk. He did the interviews for *Akenfield: Portrait of an English Village*, in 1966–7, and the book – in part a homage to Ewart Evans – was published in 1969. But it's the film based on the book, and directed by Peter Hall, that I keep returning to. *Akenfield* was released in 1974, but it was made over three years between 1970 and 1973, to be able to film during different seasons. Hall used local people as actors, who improvised their dialogue. And although I know that Jackie was living much further west in the county, where the soil and the farms and the villages are different, and although I know that he was always going to be marginal to this kind of deep-rooted agricultural community, I can't help myself from imagining him walking through the lanes and byways or cycling across the headlands in the film I can watch on my laptop.

The story is of a young man called Tom, who works as a labourer for a big farmer. The present tense of the film takes place on the day he is burying his grandfather, Old Tom, who was a labourer for the same farmer before him. The story keeps cutting back to the early years of his grandfather's life – starting work in the fields aged twelve in the early 1900s, the harshness and the poverty, Edwardian harvests, the First World War, marriage and a labourer's cottage, tied to his employ-ment on the estate, until he died. Tom is haunted by his grandfather's story of how he once tried to leave the village – of walking 40 miles to Newmarket to try to get work with the horses, and of his failure to find work, and walking 40 miles back. It is the base note to Tom's decision to reject the village, his girlfriend, his mother, and the same tied cottage that the estate landowner offers him now that his grandfather is gone. Tom won't put up with living in the afterlife of this feudal system – the cottage and the marriage that would tie him for life. He strikes out for Australia instead. It's all different and none of it is different to the West of Ireland. And it was because young men like Tom were refusing to put up with agricultural servitude that there was space for men like my uncle Jackie. Jackie was living in his own afterlife as well as the afterlife of an English rural village – it was a pale echo of the life he was sup-posed to have had, but it was at least familiar.

Family Secrets

19.

Not long ago, as I neared what I hoped were the final stages of writing this book, one of my cousins texted me a phone number that he suggested I should call. It was the number for Mary's cousin Richard on 'the other side', Lily's nephew, whom I did not know. Through the many years when I had been trying to find out about Mary and her mother, I had worried about what Lily's relatives would think if they knew what I was up to, but I had pushed the worry to the back of my mind. I knew that if they had asked me to stop, I would have felt that I must comply – so I didn't tell them. I told myself, I'm not really writing about Lily and Mary anyway, but about my grandmother and my mother and me. Which was true, but it wasn't the whole truth. Now, here was a phone number. I spent a long time looking at it, trying to summon the courage to call. How would I begin? In the end I chickened out and messaged first. A warm and friendly message came back.

Richard was living with his wife, Alison, in the house near Skibbereen where he had spent his summer holidays as a child, having inherited it a few years before from his mother, Lily's younger sister. Like me, he had been born in the 1960s and brought up in England, where his mother had trained as a nurse. And it turned out that, like me, he had been trying to uncover the story of what had happened to Lily and to Mary before he was born.

He had a copy of Mary's Funeral Mass card, the one that my aunt Peggy had shown me back in the 1990s; and he had been trying to gather information from his mother and his uncle, and from elderly friends and neighbours who might remember the events of nearly seventy years ago. He was finding it difficult to prise anything from anyone. But he had one huge advantage over me in that he remembered Lily well. She had moved to Staten Island sometime in the 1950s or 1960s, to live with an older brother, and she had settled there, returning for holidays and sometimes longer spells to see her mother. Richard knew her in those years, because each summer he would come back from London to the farm where his mother was born, to spend the school holidays loafing about, just as I and my sisters were doing a couple of miles away. But Mary was never spoken of in the house – Richard knew nothing about her until very recently. She was a missing person in both our families.

It was only after Lily died in 2018 that Richard heard she had once had a child. Through all those years Mary had been kept a secret, and now Richard was trying to recalibrate his own experience and re-examine his own memories of childhood. Were there clues to his cousin's existence that he had missed? Did Mary too visit the house in the summers, to see her mother and grandmother, and were steps taken to make sure that the two children never met? What did Mary know about Richard, the child who was allowed to belong? What did she think about him? My daughter and I paid a visit to Richard and Alison. We sat in the front room of the house in which Lily and her siblings were born and brought up, looking out over a heart-stoppingly beautiful view of the fields and the river beyond, and we felt the sadness and rage of time lost that can never be recovered.

A few months after our first meeting, Richard and Alison wrote to me. They had had the idea of tracking down Mary's death certificate. The certificate was attached to the email, and they warned me it was unpleasant reading. Mary's body was found at 192 Camberwell Grove in London on 7 January 1980, five days after she had hanged herself. The certificate described her as 'a spinster and a canteen assistant'. Here then was another secret – that Mary was not a nurse, as her family had said, and the worst thing about that secret was the fact that they had felt it was worth keeping. But it was the information that her body was undiscovered for five days that was hardest to take in. That January I was probably lying around at home, arguing with my sisters, or not doing my homework, about 12 miles away.

I arranged with Richard and Alison that we would go together to consult the record of the inquest that was held into her death, but then I discovered that Southwark Coroner's Court had not retained the files. We seem to have come to a dead end as far as records go, and all we can do now is try to account for what we have found.

It is tempting to regard this family saga as a secret history – hidden away out of shame in a chest shoved up in the attic, or buried somewhere, in a ditch or on the boundary between two fields. After all, I've had to dig. I've burrowed away in census returns, and in the registrations of births, marriages and deaths, ships' manifests, the land registry. I've upturned virtual boxes and files, sifting through the documents to scratch away at the past. And I've tried to get out of people – my aunt and uncles, and most of all my mother – what they knew, or what they can remember. It's not particularly kind, what I've been at, forcing people to look back again at all that unpleasantness.

You could think of the stories I've been telling here as the obverse of my family's secrets. Even as the death of them. In uncovering the story of what happened to my grandmother, to Lily, to Mary and to Jackie, I've been trying, on a tiny scale, to count the costs of the piety and land hunger and doomed ideals of respectability that were bolstered and enabled by the institutions of Church and state. But I've also – by default – been attacking the culture of reticence that gave people the resilience to survive. The habits of discretion and reserve that made day-to-day life liveable in a small community where everyone knew everyone else's business. It's a murderous impulse on my part, hardly heroic, even if I want to justify it on the grounds of the importance for us now of acknowledging the truth of what happened then – the need to drag it all into the open so we can't pretend we didn't know.

The trouble with this neat opposition between storytelling and secret-keeping is that it isn't true. The secrets were always embedded in the stories. Messages were always being passed. My mother learnt to read the story of her parents' marriage through the details of dates that didn't add up, and blue suits. She learnt to interpret the secret sorrows that were passed between her mother and her grandmother over Mary-that-died (even if she couldn't guess at the detail of what had happened). And she learnt that secrets were a form of care. How else to interpret her cultivation of a secret, passed on in that obscure story from Maggie and Hannah, concerning another lost baby? Making up and keeping the secret of her mother's illegitimate child – even, in the end, keeping the secret from herself – was her way of protecting her mother. It gave her a way of looking after her and it gave her a story, about her mother's vulnerability.

In the 1960s and 1970s messages were also being passed, to me and my sisters and cousins, though we didn't yet know how to interpret them. None of what happened to Lily and Mary and Jackie was really secret, except from us children, and that was only because we couldn't yet read the codes embedded in the stories we heard. But we were all living in the shadow of Lily's pregnancy, whether we knew it or not. The violence done to our absent cousin Mary shaped our lives too. It is not an exaggeration to say that it brought the family – in the sense of a group of people building a life together towards a connected future – to an end. As the family plot bought by my grandmother in the local church cemetery slowly filled with her sons, who died one after the other of ill health and hard work and alcohol poisoning in 1972, 1973 and 1976, there was no one to take their place on the farm.

Four years after my uncle Thomas keeled over in the burning summer of 1976, in June 1980, my grandmother died. She was eighty-nine years old and by now physically frail, but she wasn't, I think, confused. She will have been aware of the fact that her granddaughter Mary killed herself at the beginning of that year, though I wonder if she was able to think of her as 'my granddaughter'. Even if my aunt Peggy was careful to say nothing, she'll likely have seen the death notice in the local paper. She certainly knew that her granddaughter Caroline was pregnant that spring – they were living in the same house, and she was the one who noticed it first, pointing it out to my aunt. 'Are we expecting a wedding?' she said. When she collapsed that May, and her remaining children in England raced home to see her before it was too late, it was an echo of the 'stroke' she had had in 1954. But this time she didn't survive.

Ironically the future of the family turned out to be illegitimate. Me, my sisters and our cousins turned out to be especially good at giving birth outside marriage, and creating new families in the fissures of respectability. In this we were encouraged and supported by the surviving grown-ups – my mother and father and my uncle and aunt, who were all determined not to pass on the violence. And here it is important for me to acknowledge that the secrets that were being kept from us children were different in each generation.

What wasn't being spoken about by my grandmother during my childhood was not the same as what wasn't being spoken about by my mother and uncles and aunts. It must have seemed to my grandmother, and to Lily's parents, that the mother-and-baby home offered a way out, an opportunity for both families to ignore the problem pregnancy, and have the child adopted. Perhaps, at the start, Lily thought this was the best option too, but as the years in Bessborough and then the county home unfolded she surely changed her mind about that. And maybe her parents changed their minds, and maybe my grandmother did too. But everyone seems to have decided it was too late to do anything about it.

The passage of time has not been kind to the choices they made. It's showed them up as self-interested, short-sighted and unkind. Molly may still have thought she'd escaped from something, even if she never saw her eldest son again, and never met her grandchild. The pitiful thing is this: she was wrong. I don't mean that she was wrong in her moral assessment of Lily, or in the decision she took to value legitimate ownership of the farm above all else. That much is obvious. I mean she was wrong to imagine that she was protecting herself and the farm. It was never worth it. My Victorian grandmother avoided the indignity of having to welcome a bye-child and her mother into her home – a trial she knew all about since she had once shouldered the shame herself, and in silence. But the judgement came back in another form – as she must surely have known it would – in the shame of having cast her family out.

That was the secret our parents were keeping. They weren't bothered about legitimacy – something they proved later by welcoming and backing their children's unconventional family structures. They were hiding the shame of the violence that had been done by their parents, and their own silence in the face of that violence. By the time we were growing up in the 1960s and 1970s what couldn't be spoken of was not extra-marital sex and illegitimacy, but the terrible choices my grandmother, my uncle and the other grown-ups had made.

One of the tasks of a historian is to try to get to a place where the behaviour of people in the past begins to seem comprehensible, even natural, given the context in which they were living. The goal isn't to be able to point to the decisions people made and say, Wasn't it awful, the things that were done then? Nor, however, are historians in the business of dispensing forgiveness. I feel simultaneously admiring and wary of the fact that my mother has forgiven my grandmother, and my uncle Jackie, for what they did. One reason she chooses understanding over condemnation is surely that it costs too much not to forgive. She lost her mother and her brother, long ago. She doesn't want to lose them twice over. She wants to be able to hold her childhood – the life she had before she left home more than seventy years ago – close. What possible good would it do, at this stage, to withhold tolerance and compassion? After all, it's not as though they weren't punished.

But arguing that an individual's actions made sense, in the world they were living in, is not the same as arguing that what they did was defensible. Nor do I want to claim that my grandmother and the other grown-ups were less culpable because in sending Lily and Mary to Bessborough and the county home they did what most people at the time were doing. It's not an excuse. Nonetheless, the fact that everything I've been describing was not out of the ordinary – rather it was typical, and not merely condoned but encouraged by the institutions of Church and state – is important.

Was my Irish family really typical? Was my experience typical? The idea that my childhood in the 1960s and 1970s was, fundamentally, just like everyone else's has been a touchstone for me in writing this book. Common sense dictates I can't be right about that. I learnt my place in my Irish family at a remove. I was only home during the holidays so what can I really know of the year-long, everyday round of parents and siblings, uncles and aunts, good and bad neighbours, priests and teachers, lovers and friends? My perspective on these things is that of a person who was outside as much as inside the family. Compared to my truly rooted cousins, my experience is inauthentic, or, you might say, illegitimate. Which is, naturally, one reason why I claim it is typical.

I am aware that there's something fishy about the way that I cling to the idea that my family was the same as everybody else's. It's a useful get-out clause. What right do I have to tell these tales if they don't illuminate something larger than one family's unedifying history? I've tried to quell my doubts about spilling the beans by reminding myself that, after all, I'm not only writing about my granny and my uncles and my mother and me. We were just like the others. I've been looking for a purpose that will save me from the shame of self-exposure, and exposure of my relatives. Figures come to my rescue. From the numbers of my grandparents' siblings who emigrated to Boston in the 1890s (a good three-quarters of each labouring family's children: utterly standard), to the archetypal 30-acre farm bought in 1932 at the very moment when politicians were extolling 30 acres as the ideal farm size for the new nation, to the five out of seven siblings who emigrated to

Britain in the 1950s, to the extra-marital pregnancies, the mother-and-baby home, the county home and the industrial school – my family did the classic things, around the same time as everyone else was doing them.

It is true, of course, that no one is ever really typical. I could have told my family stories by focusing on individual inclinations, rather than shared trends: my grandfather's tendency to spout lessons from Shakespeare, learnt in his Protestant school. (He once admonished my mother for saving tuppence from the tram and spending it on sweets instead: 'He who steals my purse steals nothing . . . '); my grandmother's love of geraniums; my aunt Mary's addiction to reading romance novels; Stephen's sweet tooth. Our passions make us who we are, and I've mostly sidestepped all that. Instead, I've picked out from their stories the ways in which they were like other people. I've read my family through the lens of a 'typical' mid-century rural Irish family and it's no wonder I've found so many ways they fit the pattern: I've been looking for them. I'm not apologizing for this. It's one of the only ways I know to figure out what the pattern really is.

The most representative thing about my family was not the small farm, the nightly saying of the Rosary, or the close community of neighbours – all stereotypes with which we are overfamiliar – but the fact that most of its members lived elsewhere. Perhaps this is the biggest Irish family secret. The typical Irish family was not at home. Its members were parcelled out (voluntarily and involuntarily) to England, to America, to the schools and the institutions that taught children how to become nuns and brothers and priests, as well as to the social welfare institutions – the carceral for the carnal – that are central to the stories in this book.

There were very many differences between the two types of

institution, and one of them was that families talked about the nuns and brothers and priests (they were proud of them) and didn't talk about the others: the poor, the pregnant, the illegitimate and the mentally ill. Nor did they talk about the people who had left for England under a cloud. Either way, whether you were growing up in England or in Ireland, your family was full of gaps. That paradox – a family full of empty spaces – was lived out every day. The gaps in space and time left by those who were missing had to be filled somehow, made good, or covered over, by stories or by silence. It's these stories and silences that make my family typical. This is the way my childhood was just like everybody else's.

For a long time, I thought that what I needed to confront in telling this story was social hypocrisy, and double standards, bolstered by clerical discourses of morality and respectability, and clerical institutions. My grandmother's behaviour, and my uncle's, were explicable, perhaps, but not excusable.

But I think that what the stories of all those extra-marital pregnancies really unfolds is the meaning of what it is to know. If I look back at that photograph of our summer holiday in 1966 what I see is a group of children who didn't know that there were people missing, but who knew that something was unaccounted for – a group of children who were already, if you like, learning to read complex texts full of gaps and riddles. And behind them stand adults who knew about the missing people, indeed who were responsible for them being missing, but couldn't bear to know what they knew.

And so, the crypts. The septic tank at Tuam and the undiscovered crypt at Bessborough are full of bodies that have no records. The report of the Commission of Investigation into Mother and Baby Homes is stuffed with examples of people's refusal or inability to know what they know: nuns who signed death registrations who are unable to remember that any babies died; county council records that both acknowledge and deny awareness of what was going on in the homes. Something similar was going on in families, as the weirdly encrypted stories told in my own family show. There was violence being done to people, behind closed doors. What my grandmother's secrets reveal is the unbearable weight of the knowledge of that violence.

Acknowledgements

My debts go back a long way. Claudia FitzHerbert first encouraged me to write about this history back in the 1990s, but it took me a long time to begin. I'm grateful for many conversations over the years, especially with Claire Connolly, Vona Groarke, Fanny Howe, Paul Keegan, Siobhán Kilfeather, Caroline McCarthy, Maureen McLane, Helen Miles, Oona Roycroft, Laura Slatkin, Karen van Dyck, Anna Vaux and Frances Wilson. For research help and advice, thanks to Guy Beiner, Nicholas Canny, Caitriona Crowe, Mary Daly, Marjorie Howes, Breandán Mac Suibhne, Ian McBride, Eve Morrison, Neel Mukherjee, Margaret Murphy of the Skibbereen Heritage Centre, Katherine O'Donnell, Conall Ó Fátharta, Eunan O'Halpin, Ian Patterson, Alexandra Poulain, James Smith and Finbarr Whooley. Thanks to Joe Nugent for the joyous field trip to Marblehead and Peabody, and to Vera Kreilkamp for insisting we ignore the barbed wire.

I had the great good fortune to spend a year as a Fellow at the Columbia Institute for Ideas and Imagination in Paris, where I completed a first draft of this book, and I would especially like to thank Marie D'Origny, Carol Gluck, Mark Mazower, Yasmine El Rashidi and the 2021–22 cohort of fellows for their readings, discussion and support. Thanks too to my wonderful agent Sarah Chalfant, to Simon Winder, Eva Hodgkin, Charlotte Ridings and everyone at Penguin Allen Lane, and to Jonathan Galassi and Katie Liptak at Farrar, Straus and Giroux. Chapters 4 and 5 are revised versions of an essay published in the *New York Review of Books* in 2018, with thanks to my editor Jana Prikryl. Thanks to Joanne O'Leary and Alice Spawls at the *London Review of Books* for the opportunity to write about the *Final Report of the Commission of Investigation into the Mother and Baby Homes*, in 'Architectures of Containment', May 2021.

Richard and Alison Northam showed astounding kindness and generosity to a stranger, and I am immensely grateful to them for the trust they placed in me. My principal thanks are to the family members who are listed at the front of this book: my mother and her siblings Peggy and Jimmy, my sisters, my children, and my cousins Caroline, Cormac, Fergus, Jenny, Kevin, Paula, Shane and Timmy. This story is as much theirs as mine, and I thank them for allowing me to tell it here.

Images

p. v: Giovanni Bellini, *Madonna Adoring the Sleeping Child*, early 1460s. The Metropolitan Museum of Art, Theodore M. Davis Collection, Bequest of Theodore M. Davis, 1915.

p. 14: In front of the farmhouse, 1966. Left to right: Philly, Molly holding Oona, Clair, Siobhan, Stephen, Bridget.

p. 38: Clair with her mother Philly, and a donkey, in the back yard, 1966.

p. 40: Uncle Stephen in the late 1960s.

p. 66: Philly and Molly in the early 1950s.

p. 111: Great-uncle Jack, a tintype photograph made in America, early 1890s.

p. 147: Philly and her brother Jimmy, snapped by a street photographer on Patrick Street in Cork, early 1950s.

p. 160: Still from *Radharc Oldbury Camp 1965*. Copyright © The Radharc Trust.

p. 163: Jack MacGowran in Samuel Beckett's *Eh Joe*, 1966. Copyright © BBC Archive.